The People of the Plains

Dedication to the 1909 Edition

To
The Right Honourable Earl Grey, G.C.M.G., G.C.V.W.
Governor-General
and
Commander-in-Chief of the Dominion of Canada
This volume
is
by Gracious Permission of His Excellency
Respectfully Inscribed

The People of the Plains

by Amelia M. Paget

with a new Introduction by Sarah Carter

2004

UNIVERSITY OF
REGINA

CANADIAN PLAINS
RESEARCH CENTER

Canadian Plains Research Center
University of Regina
Regina, Saskatchewan S4S 0A2
Canada
Tel: (306) 585-4758
Fax: (306) 585-4699
e-mail: canadian.plains@uregina.ca
http://www.cprc.uregina.ca

Library and Archives Canada Cataloguing in Publication

Paget, Amelia M.
The people of the plains / by Amelia Paget ; with a new introduction by Sarah Carter.

(Canadian Plains reprint series, ISSN 1208-9680 ; 11)
First published: Toronto : W. Briggs, 1909.
Includes bibliographical references and index.
ISBN 0-88977-159-6

1. Cree Indians. 2. Ojibwa Indians. 3. Indians of North America--Prairie Provinces. 4. Northwest, Canadian. 5. Qu'Appelle River Valley (Sask. and Man.) I. University of Regina. Canadian Plains Research Center. II. Title. III. Series.

E78.C2P13 2004   971.2004'97323   C2004-905006-0

Cover design by Donna Achtzehner, Canadian Plains Research Center
Cover image by Geraldine Moodie, June 1895: "Distant view of the Sun Dance encampment showing the main tent to the left with other tents surrounding it, especially to the right."
Printed and bound in Canada by Houghton Boston, Saskatoon
Index prepared by Patricia Furdek (www.userfriendlyindexes.com)

We acknowledge the financial support of the Government of Canada through the Book Publishing Industry Development Program (BPIDP) for our publishing activities.

Contents

Introduction to the 2004 Edition

by Sarah Carter

The "Cordial Advocate": Amelia McLean Paget and *The People of the Plains*

WHILE IN OTTAWA IN 1911 THE BRITISH TRAVEL WRITER and Fellow of the Royal Anthropological Institute, Bessie Pullen-Burry, was pleased to secure an introduction to Amelia Paget (née McLean), the author of "a valuable work entitled *The People of the Plains*, in which she describes sympathetically and graphically the life, customs, with their religious beliefs, of the Crees and Saulteaux, her life-long friends, to whom she is devoted; their gentle and dignified manners are to her their striking characteristic."[1] Pullen-Burry admired Paget not only because of her book but because of her intriguing family background, noting that her maternal family had for several generations held positions in the Hudson's Bay Company (HBC), that she had been born at a northern trading post, and that during the Métis Resistance of 1885 she and her family had been captives of "hostile Indians," their eventual release coming about "through the intervention of friendly Indians." When asked of this experience Paget told her visitor that "I have heard of savage, revengeful cruelties, but I have never seen that side of Indian nature, and speak as I find."

Amelia Paget defied and complicated colonial categories and divides in her book *The People of the Plains*, published in 1909.[2] As a person of part-Aboriginal ancestry she also complicated boundaries of identity and difference.[3] She was not radically subversive and outspoken however, never providing a sustained or strident indictment of prevailing assumptions and the effects of colonialism. She was a "cordial advocate," for Aboriginal people, as poet and Department of Indian Affairs bureaucrat Duncan Campbell Scott described Paget in the introduction to her book, rather than a "frigid critic" of colonialism.[4]

The People of the Plains directly challenged negative representations and distortions of Aboriginal people by providing sympathetic and nuanced descriptions of their spirituality, community life, language, humour, music, artistry and oral culture.[5] The book should be understood in part within the context of the American writers analysed by Sherry L. Smith in her recent book *Reimagining Indians: Native Americans Through Anglo Eyes, 1890–1940*.[6] At the turn of the twentieth century a number of Anglo men and women including George Bird Grinnell, Walter McClintock, Frank Bird Linderman, and Mary Roberts Rinehart became captivated by Native American cultures, and were determined to fashion new, positive images. They urged their readers to cast aside the prejudice, ignorance and hostility that prevailed at that time among non-Aboriginal people. Smith writes that "In encouraging their countrymen to understand and sympathize with Indians, they both championed the distinctions of Indians' cultures while simultaneously insisting on their shared humanity."[7] They produced books for popular audiences that "offered new ways to conceptualize Indian people, alternatives to the images that had transfixed Americans for centuries."[8] In stressing the richness and value of the cultures and communities of Plains people, Amelia Paget encouraged her readers to rethink derogatory attitudes and to have greater compassion, tolerance and generosity.

Paget's background made her quite distinct from other champions of Aboriginal people such as Grinnell, McClintock, Linderman and Rinehart. She was born in the North-West, unlike the other authors who travelled west with the intention of discovering "exotics" and becoming immersed in an "alien" culture. She was raised at HBC posts and was fluent in Aboriginal languages. She experienced first-hand times of great upheaval in Western Canada. In 1885 Amelia McLean and her teenage sisters Eliza and Kitty were briefly national celebreties during their family's two months' residence with Plains Cree chief Big Bear and a mobile group of Plains and Woods Cree. The McLean family was involved in three violent confrontations during 1885 at Fort Pitt, Frenchman Butte and Steele's Narrows.

Also distinguishing Paget from the other authors is the fact that her great-great-grandmother was an Aboriginal woman. This is not mentioned in *The People of the Plains*, or any other McLean family memoirs. Like members of other fur-trade, mixed-ancestry families of the later nineteenth century, the McLeans did not acknowledge, and even took steps to obliterate this heritage. In the obituary for Paget's grandmother Anne Campbell Murray, for example, it was stated that she was born at Fort Dunvegan in 1822 and that she was "the first white child to claim those distant northwestern regions as a birthplace."[9] Yet in 1876, Anne Campbell Murray applied for and received Métis scrip.[10] Many other of Paget's relatives similarly received Métis scrip, including her great-uncle Duncan Campbell, great-aunt Magdaline Bunn (née Campbell), aunts Flora Murray, Eliza McDonald (née Murray), Jemima Bedson (née Murray) and her five children, Paget's cousins.[11] While this Aboriginal ancestry was somewhat distant by the time of Amelia McLean Paget's generation, it was not forgotten or ignored by others who identified her family as "half-breeds." Artist Edmund Morris, who was acquainted with fur-trade families from his childhood in Winnipeg (his father Alexander Morris was Lieutenant-Governor of Manitoba and the North-West Territories), wrote in his 1909 diary after receiving a copy of *The People of the Plains*, that it was "By Mrs. Padgett [sic], whose grandmother was one of the Dog Ribb [sic] [Dene] Indians. She is related to the Campbells & Murrays—half breeds."[12] Although Morris had details of Paget's ancestry wrong, this notation indicates how the McLeans and their relatives were perceived. Paget had highly personal reasons, then, for countering derogatory contemporary representations of Aboriginal people.

It would not be appropriate, however, to view Amelia Paget as a woman "ahead of her time," in her positive portrayal of Plains Aboriginal people, nor does she provide readers with an unproblematic "authentic" insider's perspective by virtue of her ancestry.[13] Her book reveals that she was not able to depart from the influence of

ideas and attitudes about vanishing Aboriginal people that were
current in her day. While her
book celebrated Plains culture, it
also conveyed the idea that much
had disappeared, diminished or
been altered forever. The goal of
the book was to capture a portrait
of this life before it faded. There
was also distance between author
and subject despite her close
acquaintances and knowledge of
languages. At HBC posts there
was a distinct hierarchy and the
McLean family would have
enjoyed elite status and treatment. As the memoirs of her sister Kitty suggest, the McLean
children learned most of what
they knew about Aboriginal people through their servants and
nursemaids. As in a Victorian
middle-class home, servants did
not enjoy the status of family
members. The McLean children
would have been protected from,
and often oblivious to, much of
the world beyond the stockade of
the trading post.

Amelia Anne McLean was
born in 1867 at Fort Simpson
(present-day Northwest Territories), a fur-trading post situated

Western Canada Pictorial Index 0248-07923

William J. McLean, Amelia's father.

on an island at the confluence of the Mackenzie (Dehcho) and Liard (Naechagah)
rivers.[14] For hundreds of years this had been an important rendezvous site for the
Dene, who called it Liidli Kue, or the place where the rivers come together.[15]
Amelia's family had a long association with this and other fur-trading posts of the
Mackenzie and Athabaska districts. She was the eldest of 12 children born to HBC
employee William J. McLean, who was from the Isle of Lewis, Scotland, and Helen
Hunter Murray. Amelia's parents exemplified the marriage pattern of the previous
generations in which the men came from away, (Scotland and in one case Upper
Canada), and the women were born and raised in the north. Amelia's mother Helen
was born in 1847, likely at La Pierre's House on Bell River, and she grew up at Fort
Yukon, Fort Simpson and later at the southern posts of Fort Garry (Winnipeg),
Pembina and Fort Georgetown (Minnesota). She was the daughter of the founder of
Fort Yukon, HBC chief trader Alexander Hunter Murray, who was from Kilmun,
Argyllshire, Scotland and Anne Campbell, mentioned above, one of many children

Western Canada Pictorial Index 0631-19534

Helen (née Hunter Murray) McLean, Amelia's mother.

born to Elizabeth McGillivray and Chief Trader of the Athabasca District Colin Campbell, who was from Upper Canada.[16]

Elizabeth McGillivray was the daughter of an Aboriginal woman and Scotsman John McGillivray of the North West Company (NWC). The nation to which John McGillivray's Aboriginal wife belonged is not certain, but she was likely Woods Cree. They were married *à la façon du pays* around 1796 when McGillivray was serving in the Lower English (Churchill) River department, which was Woods Cree territory.[17] They had one son, William, as well as Elizabeth. More is known about William than his sister. William is identified in HBC Governor Sir George Simpson's character book as "A half breed of the Cree nation."[18] He was educated in Montreal for four years and returned to work first for the NWC and then the HBC as a clerk at Fort Chipewyan and later in New Caledonia.[19] William married a daughter of Chief Trader Alexander Stewart and Susan Spence. He drowned in the Fraser River in January, 1832.[20] (When William and Elizabeth's father John McGillivray retired from the NWC in 1818 he settled in Upper Canada, married for a second time and had a family of eight.[21] These children would have been nearly the same age as his grand-children born to Elizabeth and Colin Campbell.)

While for several generations Amelia's family was located in the Mackenzie and Athabaska districts, there were close ties and associations with the Red River Settlement. In the 1850s Colin and Elizabeth Campbell sent nine daughters, pre-sumably one of which was Amelia's grandmother Anne, to Red River all at the same time, to attend school. There was "a boatload of handsome young girls," according to one account.[22] Anne Campbell and Alexander Murray's children also went to school at Red River. The daughters including Helen, attended Miss Davis's School and the sons St. John's College.[23] The trip from Fort Simpson to Red River, that Amelia and earlier generations of her family would have made, is vividly described in the book *Women of Red River*. Nineteen-year old Sarah Foulds made the journey in 1868, leaving on June 4 by York boat from Lower Fort Garry and arriving at Fort Simpson on August 18:

> We went down the Red to Lake Winnipeg, up the Lake to Grand Rapids, where the Saskatchewan river, after seven miles of rapids, empties into the Lake. There we had to make our first portage. The boats were taken over on low cars drawn by horses

along a narrow little wooden railway from the Lake to above the rapids. There they were put into the Saskatchewan river and started on the long journey to Portage la Loche, or the Long Portage, as it used to be called, which was a portage over the height of land dividing the drainage areas of the two great river systems between the Hudson Bay and the Rocky Mountains. That portage was sixteen miles long. The boat brigade which had brought us more than eleven hundred miles from Fort Garry turned back there. When we had crossed Portage la Loche we had entered the basin of the Mackenzie river system, which empties into the Arctic ocean. There were ponies and oxen and carts to carry the freight across to the end of the portage, where the brigade of boats from the Mackenzie river was waiting for us. And then we had nearly a thousand miles more to travel with the Mackenzie boats before we arrived at Fort Simpson.[24]

Amelia's earliest years to 1873 were spent at Fort Liard, North West Territories, where her father was clerk-in-charge. W.J. McLean was transferred to Fort Qu'Appelle in 1873 and his family joined him there one year later. The post was situated in the beautiful Qu'Appelle Valley, formed by an ancient meandering river that is framed by deep ravines, gentle hills and wooded coulees.[25] For generations of Aboriginal people the Qu'Appelle Valley has been a treasured gathering place, an oasis because of its generally abundant and varied resources. In the late 1850s explorer H.Y. Hind found clear evidence of the antiquity of the Qu'Appelle Valley as a gathering place as he found numerous remains of encampments that he thought must have been used for centuries. The Qu'Appelle Valley was also a place of great spiritual significance and attachment dating to ancient times. The Moose Bay burial mound, on the crest of a high rim of the Qu'Appelle commanding a majesterial view of the river with Crooked Lake directly below, has been dated to AD 1040.[26]

To the Plains Cree this was the valley of the What is Calling River, in Cree *ka-tepwewi-sipiy*.[27] The Calling River Cree, or *ka-tepwewi-sipiyiniwak*, a branch of the Plains Cree, had a deep and long-standing attachment to this river valley. In Aaron Arrowsmith's 1814 map of North America the river is clearly identified as the territory of the Calling River Cree.[28] The name is derived from the way that sounds echo and reverberate in the valley, and there are many stories about the spirit that travelled the river calling with a human voice. Amelia Paget told several of the legends of the spirit of the valley in *The People of the Plains*:

> One of the prettiest of the many traditions relating to the valley was that of the young woman who, imagining her lover was calling to her from one of the hills, pushed off in her little bark canoe and was never heard of any more. Her voice was left in the valley and answers back in plaintive tones when anyone calls. Her lover returned a short time after her departure, but, though he followed her, never found even a trace of her canoe. At twilight her canoe would appear for a few minutes upon the surface of one of the many beautiful lakes in the valley, only to disappear again in a soft mist if anyone tried to approach it.[29]

By the 1870s the Qu'Appelle Valley was also home to some Saulteaux (Plains Ojibway), and there were many mixed Plains Cree and Saulteaux bands. One of the largest of the Qu'Appelle bands in the 1870s, led by Chief Piapot, was mixed Cree and Assiniboine. Groups of Dakota and Métis were also occupants of the Qu'Appelle Valley. The reserves surveyed closest to Fort Qu'Appelle in the 1870s were Piapot, Pasquah (Saulteaux and Cree), Muscowpetung (Saulteaux) and Standing Buffalo (Dakota).

The McLeans' arrival at Fort Qu'Appelle coincided with a period of unprecedented, momentous change and turmoil. In 1869–70 the vast expanse of territory known to fur traders as "Rupert's Land" was transferred to the new Dominion of Canada, and ambitious plans were in the works to build a railway and settle the west with agriculturalists. By the 1870s buffalo had all but vacated the Qu'Appelle Valley and the staple of the plains economy collapsed. In September of 1874 the Cree, Saulteaux and Assinboine nations of this region negotiated Treaty Four at Fort Qu'Appelle, ushering in the era of reserves, government administration and efforts to create a new economy based on agriculture. (Helen McLean was one of the witnesses who signed Treaty Four.) The North-West Mounted Police (NWMP) were created in 1873 and were dispatched on their famous "March West" in the summer of 1874, travelling through Treaty Four territory before the treaty was made that fall. In 1875 a police detachment was located at Swan River, briefly the capital of the North-West.

W.J. McLean took over from Isaac Cowie as the clerk-in-charge at Fort Qu'Appelle and in his memoirs Cowie described "the pleasure of meeting his good wife and fine family of little children [four at that time], whose rosy appearance reflected great credit on their place of birth, in McKenzie River."[30] During their Fort Qu'Appelle years the McLeans had four more children. The HBC first established a trading post in the Qu'Appelle in 1854 (Qu'Appelle Lakes Post) and by the time of the arrival of the McLeans, Fort Qu'Appelle was a substantial establishment of seven houses, trading, fur and provision stores surrounded by a stockade. During Isaac Cowie's residence there in a typical winter (1867–68) he described a lively settlement of over 16 engaged servants (clerks, interpreters, bowman, watchman, middleman, carpenter, cattlekeeper, woodcutter, voyageurs and labourers) with 11 wives, 20 children and 30 train dogs.[31] The servants and their families were mostly Métis, Saulteaux, and Cree, while the clerks, traders and chief factors were from Scotland.

W.J. McLean was promoted to Junior Chief Trader in 1877 and to Chief Trader in 1880, so that by that time he and his family occupied the top rung of the social ladder of the establishment. HBC posts were not egalitarian settings. There were many ways in which ordinary workers were distinguished from their superiors. W.A. Griesbach, who was born at Fort Qu'Appelle in 1878, described the eating arrangements that reinforced the sense of social station that was observed at HBC posts: "At the 'Big House' three tables were set for each meal. At the first table was the MacLean [sic] family and such officers as might be about. The second table was for clerks and traders and the third table there was a sort of free-for-all for people of lesser degree."[32]

Amelia's younger sister Kitty (Kate Flora, born in 1871) wrote a memoir that featured the Fort Qu'Appelle years, and she described a nearly idyllic setting for children.[33] In winter they coasted on sleds and on their moccasined feet, and went cariole driving. In summer they tramped in the woods, and rode after wild horses. Among the highlights of the Fort Qu'Appelle years was greeting a contingent of newly minted NWMP upon their arrival in the West. According to Kitty's account it was Helen McLean who trained Aboriginal women of Fort Qu'Appelle to cut and sew the first buffalo coats for the police. The McLeans also met the famous Lakota Chief Sitting Bull who visited Fort Qu'Appelle. The children became well-acquainted with the people, customs and languages of the Plains Cree and Saulteaux, forming friendships and

Western Canada Pictorial Index 0248-07924

The McLean family, c. 1895. Left to right, top row: Helen (Sapomin), Duncan, Kitty, William; middle row: Freda, John, Eliza, Angus, Amelia; bottom row: Murray, Lillian, Lawrence.

attending special events and ceremonies in their communities. Some of the children were "adopted" by Aboriginal people. An old woman named "Appearing Over the Hill," adopted Kitty and helped an injury to her knee to heal.[34] Duncan, born in 1877, was adopted by a couple who had a son born to them the same day but the infant had not survived for long.[35] Every year until they left the Fort this couple and their relatives brought gifts for Duncan. According to Kitty, the children learned the languages through their maids.[36] One of their housemaids was named "Eloquent Speaker" and she was a daughter of the prominent Saulteaux Chief Pasquah, one of the Treaty Four chiefs. The McLean girls also became proficient riders and they learned to shoot. They were not allowed to go any distance from the Fort without their rifles. Kitty described her sister Amelia on one occasion being chased by a timber wolf when some distance from the Fort:

> *She was the eldest of my sisters, and though often called "the brave one" she found her bravery was not sufficient on this occasion to face a huge timber wolf. So she ran as hard as she could, reaching the gate of the Fort and slamming it just in time!*[37]

Kitty's memoirs emphasized the positive side of life at Fort Qu'Appelle; there is almost no indication that they were living in the midst of Cree and Saulteaux territory at a time of great destitution and distress for these nations. Conditions were grim by the late 1870s, as environmental conditions and the government's failure to provide the assistance promised under treaty resulted in little progress in agriculture.[38]

There was widespread suffering and many deaths from disease. In the winter of 1878, 75 people were found starving on the plains 50 miles south of Fort Qu'Appelle.[39] They camped near the fort that winter, which was severe, and toward spring they all contracted a fatal disease and died within three or four days. The first farm instructor to the reserves near Fort Qu'Appelle found in the winter of 1879-80 that the people were suffering greatly, showing clear signs of starvation. The children, he reported were *"really* crying for food."[40] Housed behind the stockade of the Fort it is possible that the McLean children were not aware of the extent of the suffering around them.

The older McLean children spent the winter months of their later Fort Qu'Appelle years at school at Red River, by that time known as Winnipeg. The girls attended the Anglican St. John's College Ladies School in Winnipeg. The register of attendance and conduct for 1881 of this school indicates that Amelia and her sister Eliza (b. 1869) were in the same class and they took scripture, composition, object lessons, geography, poetry, reading, writing, spelling, French and English history.[41] Amelia was first in the class and Eliza second. Their classmates were other children of prominent fur trade families with last names such as Rowand, Begg, Pritchard, Norquay and Bruce. The McLean girls had many relatives in Winnipeg and they would have been part of an elite of the old fur trade set that was rapidly being displaced by new business and industrial elites. Their grandfather Alexander Hunter Murray, who had been in charge of Lower Fort Garry and had designed the gates of the Upper Fort (that still stand near the Forks of the Red and the Assiniboine in downtown Winnipeg), died in 1874, but their grandmother Anne lived until 1907 at their home, "Bellevue," a mile below Lower Fort Garry. According to Kitty's memoirs many distinguished guests were entertained at Bellevue over the years including General Garnet Wolseley, Lord Minto and the poet John Greenleaf Whittier.[42]

In 1884 W.J. McLean was appointed Chief Trader at Fort Pitt, a small HBC post consisting of a few buildings forming a square, and situated on the North Saskatchewan River, in the parkland region at the intersection of the territory of the Plains Cree and the Woods Cree. The McLean children spent their first and only winter at Fort Pitt riding, snowshoeing, coasting, and on rifle and revolver practice. They also had music, cards and occasional dances. Amelia would entertain at times by translating songs into Cree or Saulteaux.[43] In the world just beyond Fort Pitt it was a winter of hardship and rising tensions. The arrival of the McLeans coincided with that of the Plains Cree chief Big Bear and his approximately 500 followers to the Fort Pitt and Frog Lake district. In 1876, when Treaty Six was made with the Plains Cree and Assiniboine at Forts Carlton and Pitt, Big Bear, a distinguished leader with a following of approximately 2,000, refused to adhere. He initially wanted to see if the government would keep its side of the bargain, and he then wanted to negotiate better terms. He only agreed to take the treaty in 1882 following years of meagre subsistence for his followers, many of whom had dispersed, while others questioned and challenged his leadership.

In the fall of 1884 Big Bear was obliged to choose a reserve in the Frog Lake district near the government agency that served the 500 Woods Cree resident there, but arrangements had not been finalized. It was a winter of great want and discontent as the food resources of the district were strained.[44] On the morning of April 2, 1885, nine men, including government employees and two priests, were killed at Frog Lake by some Plains Cree men of Big Bear's band. This event took place after a March 26 confrontation at Duck Lake, between NWMP and Métis of nearby Batoche and St. Laurent, that left 15 dead. A massive mobilization of troops for the North-West campaign began with word of Duck Lake. Non-Aboriginal people from surrounding settlements sought the safety of Fort Pitt in the light of these events. Many of them were escorted there by Cree friends and associates who feared for their safety in that climate of tension.[45] There were 67 people then housed at Fort Pitt, including a contingent of 23 NWMP under the command of Francis Dickens (son of the famous novelist Charles Dickens). Sentries were posted around the buildings and the three eldest McLean girls, including 18-year old Amelia, took their turns at sentry duty. (A depiction of this scene was featured in the *Montreal Daily Star*

Image from the Montreal Daily Star, *May 23, 2885. The original caption read: "Noble Women on the Defensive: The Misses McLean show great courage, each one rifle in hand, stands at a loophole."*

of May 23, 1885 with the caption "Noble Women on the Defensive: The Misses McLean show great courage, each one rifle in hand, stands at a loophole."

On April 14 Fort Pitt was visited by Big Bear and about 250 Cree, and W.J. McLean was requested to meet with them at the Cree camp. Two days of consultation followed and these were interrupted by a violent confrontation that began when it appeared to the Cree that they were under attack. One policemen was killed and another seriously wounded. The wounded man was successfully brought into Fort Pitt while Amelia and others provided covering fire. Three Cree were killed during this confrontation. Concerned about their father after these events, Amelia and Kitty left the fort on foot and walked unescorted into the Cree camp. According to McLean family accounts, some of the Cree were astonished at their nerve, and asked if they were afraid. In her perfect Cree Amelia replied: "Why should we be afraid of you? We have lived together as brothers and sisters for years. We speak the same language. Why should we be afraid of you?"[46] The sisters returned with a message that Cree chief Wandering Spirit had McLean write, requesting that the rest of the McLeans and other occupants join the Cree camp.

Under the leadership of W.J. McLean, the people housed at Fort Pitt (not including the NWMP who were allowed to depart for Fort Battleford) agreed that they would evacuate the fort and join the Cree camp. For the next two months the

Glenbow Archives

Fort Pitt being evacuated by Inspector F. Dickens and detachment of NWMP, 1885.

McLean family travelled with the Cree and they endured many hardships including a lack of food, miserable weather and menacing, threatening behaviour from some of their hosts. Helen McLean was pregnant with her tenth child, Freda, who was born later that year. The group first travelled to Frog Lake to meet up with the remainder of Big Bear's camp which by this time contained a great number of the Aboriginal and non-Aboriginal residents of the surrounding settlements. These included two widows of Frog Lake, Theresa Delaney and Theresa Gowanlock. Concern for the safety of the two widows, and rumours of their ill-treatment, reached hysterical proportions that spring. About the end of April the camp moved to Frenchman Butte, where on May 28 there was a confrontation with the pursuing Field Force. From there the Cree camp moved in a northeasterly direction and it was here that the McLean family endured some of their most trying conditions, including having to cross a mile-wide muskeg at one point that successfully halted the Field Force pursuit. There was a confrontation with the NWMP under the command of Inspector S.B. Steele at the narrows of Makwa Lake during which five Cree were killed and two NWMP scouts wounded. The shots fired by the police endangered the McLean family, as did the deaths of the Cree, as there were some who began to talk about taking revenge against people in their camp. On June 15 the McLeans were allowed to leave the Cree and they arrived back at Fort Pitt on June 22.

During their months with the Cree rumours had circulated that the older McLean girls were being mistreated, that they had been made "slaves of the lesser chiefs," and had suffered the "final outrage."[47] They were not, however, the objects of the same level of frenzied attention that was directed toward the two White widows of Frog Lake, Theresa Delaney and Theresa Gowanlock. As I have argued in the book *Capturing Women*, the resilience and resourcefulness of the McLeans, their shooting skills, courage and independence did not conform to prevailing expectations of White women as weak, vulnerable and passive. There was also the issue of their Aboriginal ancestry which complicated their perceived need to be "rescued from the Indians" in the same way as the two Theresas. When the family arrived at Battleford late in June of 1885, a policeman described Helen McLean as a "thin woman with Indian blood in her veins."[48]

Rumours of their mistreatment and even demise (Eliza recalled that all of the McLeans' relatives thought they had perished and had spent many tearful hours

Western Canada Pictorial Index 0248-07921

Eliza McLean at the ruins of Fort Ellice.

making mourning clothes) proved untrue. Once they emerged from their ordeal correspondents commented at length on the fortitude of the McLean girls. They were all reported to be strong and healthy, particularly Amelia, who was descried as "plucky enough for life guardsmen."[49] She was praised for her courage, especially for having shouldered a Winchester and taken her turn at sentry duty. Amelia was quoted as saying that she "would not have believed the endurance they all manifested possible, but now looks back at most of it with enjoyment." One of the McLean girls told a correspondent that although she was glad to have her life among the Indians at an end, she had "rather enjoyed the trip as a whole. She appeared inclined to look upon their experience as a joke."[50] Members of the Alberta Field Force who went to the rescue of the McLeans were apparently disappointed that the young women had not displayed more gratitude. According to one account,

> Instead of the young ladies rushing promiscuously into the arms of the soldiers, calling them their deliverers and rewarding the best looking with heart and hand, they took the matter very coolly [sic] and seemed ... if the scouts are to be believed ... to regret rather than otherwise having been compelled, through vulgar scarcity of grub, to sever their connections with their Indian friends. Apparently the blood-thirsty Indians had not been altogether unsusceptible to the charms of the prisoners, and instead of maltreating them, or hanging their gory scalps on lodge poles, they used them with all possible consideration...[51]

In the American West, women like Amelia and her sisters might have enjoyed greater and more longlasting fame (as "Amelia-Get-Your-Gun" for example), but little attention was paid to them after the spring of 1885. A book published in London, England in 1896 called *The Red House by the Rockies: A Tale of Riel's Rebellion*, by Anne Mercier and Violet Watt was about the events of 1885 in Saskatchewan, despite the title, and it featured the story of the McLeans, although the name was changed to McIntosh. This change of name was explained in the introduction which praised the "valour and pious courage shown by [W.J. McLean], his wife, and daughters, [which] are matters of history." Any hints of Aboriginal family connections were removed. The dark-haired McLean girls were given a different appearance. There are only two daughters in the story, and the eldest has become Maggie, "a typical Scotch lassie, freckled, sandy, with high cheek-bones, and no charm but a look of honest sense and good nature."[52]

Aside from *The Red House by the Rockies*, the adventures of Amelia and her sisters during 1885 garnered little attention. Following the events of that year the family lived quietly at Lower Fort Garry where W.J. McLean was in charge of the Lake Winnipeg district (1886-93). There were compelling reasons for the McLeans to avoid the limelight after 1885. Sylvia Van Kirk has described the "particular tragedy of the 'British-Indian'people of Rupert's Land [which] was that, in the end they were neither white nor Métis."[53] They tried to disappear into the White world, but were never fully accepted or included in that select category; they were seen as "white but not quite."[54] In Western Canada they were identified by many as "half-breeds." British traveller Peter O'Leary noted for example, while at Red River in 1874 that "Several white men, including some of the leading citizens, are married to half-breeds..."[55] He wrote that "Some of those women are very handsome, combining the delicacy and grace of the whites, with the dignity and keen perception of the Indians." But "half-breeds" were typically described as deficient in comparison to non-Aboriginal newcomers. O'Leary described their "social habits" as "very primitive and simple," and noted that "they are fond of excitement, such as hunting, whiskey drinking and going to balls and parties..."

The events of 1885 further intensified colonial racial categorization and shattered hopes for a more inclusive and tolerant nation.[56] Aboriginal people were viewed as a threat to the property and safety of the non-Aboriginal newcomers, who took steps to enhance segregation. It increasingly became a social and economic liability to be of mixed ancestry. The Métis had led two resistances and were perceived as a dangerous, sinister influence. As Ann Laura Stoler has written, in colonial contexts Métis people "ambiguously straddled, crossed, and threatened" imperial divides and colonial categories. Métissage was "Conceived as a dangerous source of subversion, it was seen as a threat to white prestige, an embodiment of European degeneration and moral decay."[57] Discourses of racial and social purity, that warned of the threats of decline and pollution of the imperial race, characterized English-Canadian constructions of national identity in the 1880s.[58] At this time throughout the British Empire there was a pervasive anxiety about imperial degeneration, and concern to enhance racial renewal through purity campaigns. Powerfully negative images of Aboriginal women, that served to symbolize the shortcomings of their societies, were assiduously promoted during and after 1885. They were depicted as abused and overworked drudges in their own communities, and as a source of immorality, vice and corruption in the new White communities. These negative images of Aboriginal women combined with anxieties about the perils of racial mixing and concerns about threats to the purity and sanctity of White women. (Illustrating these "dangers," and complicating colonial categories in the West, was the fact that the woman often celebrated as the "first White woman" in the West, Marie-Anne Gaboury Lagimodiere, was Louis Riel's grandmother.[59])

Negative representations of Aboriginal women, concerns about racial mixing, and intolerant attitudes were extraordinarily resilient, persisting well into the next century. They pervaded "society" at the highest level in Canada and the British Empire. In 1901 Governor General Lord Minto expressed his scorn for Lady Strathcona, the wife of Lord Strathcona (Donald A. Smith). The former Isabelle Hardisty had, like Paget, an Aboriginal foremother. Minto was highly critical of "poor old Strathcona attempting to lead society[,] the ways of which he is ignorant of, with a squaw wife who is absolutely hopeless what could he expect."[60] These attitudes also permeated the work of poet Duncan Campbell Scott. While there is debate about Scott's attitudes toward Aboriginal people as expressed in his poems, there is no doubt that he articulated his concern about the dangers of racial mixing in poems that feature Aboriginal women as remnants of their nations.[61] In the "Onondaga Madonna," (1894) and "The Half-Breed Girl" (1906) Scott associated racial mixing with decline and despair.[62] According to one critic "Onondaga Madonna" is about "the tragic confusion of the *métis* … the general tragedy of all blood-mixture."[63] The "Half-breed Girl" is tormented and haunted by her mixed ancestry. There is "something behind her savage life/ [that] shines like a fragile veil." According to Stan Dragland "That something, 'what she knows and knows not,' is her Scottish heritage. It torments her because she senses it without being able to identify what it is…"[64]

Living in Winnipeg after 1885, Amelia McLean worked occasionally for the federal Indian Affairs department, as her language skills were highly valued.[65] Duncan Campbell Scott praised her linguistic skills in his introduction to *The People of the Plains*, writing that she was "gifted with a language-sense which made possible a knowledge of the subtlest peculiarities of two languages, the Cree and Ojibway, both highly expressive, but the last eminently flexible and poetic."[66] Amelia McLean would have known Scott from at least 1899, when she married Frederick Paget, who was at that time just appointed chief accountant of the Department of Indian Affairs in Ottawa. Frederick Paget had worked in the Regina office of the department as assistant to Indian Commissioners Hayter Reed and Amédée Forget.[67] Although an accountant, Paget was also valued for his advice on Western Indians, and in this regard his wife would have been an asset. He was the author in 1908 of a lengthy report on residential schools in the West based on his own inspection, which was highly critical of the condition of many school buildings and of the quality of the staff.[68] The Pagets had one child, a daughter, Helen Charlotte (Holmes).

In 1906, Amelia Paget received a small commission from the Department of Indian Affairs to interview Plains Elders concerning their history, customs and folklore. As Duncan Campbell Scott explained in the introduction to the book, the small commission was for the "purpose of gleaning such memories as remain of the bygone domestic life of the western tribes…"[69] The project was initiated by the Governor General of Canada, Earl Grey. As explained in a newspaper report:

> His excellency the governor general who has taken a great interest in the Cree
> Indians, their mode of living and their history, ever since his visit to the northwest
> a year ago, is most anxious that the annals, lore and traditions of this decreasing but

interesting race should be preserved and handed down to posterity, and in order to do this, he has made arrangements with the Dominion government to send out a special emissary to obtain the requisite information.[70]

It was further noted that Amelia Paget had been chosen to undertake this task, as it was necessary to find someone with "a complete mastery of the Cree language, as well as clear insight into and knowledge of the Indian character." It was not certain at this point that a book would result from this fieldwork, only that "The information and interesting data thus gained will be preserved in the archives of the Indian department and no doubt will be an important factor in histories yet to be written." Earl Grey apparently did not perceive that a book would result from this research, as he only grudgingly allowed *The People of the Plains* to be dedicated to him in 1909, writing that he could not refuse to accept and "I confess, however, to a feeling of surprise that this report of Mrs. Paget's has developed into a publication which justifies such a dedication."[71]

Amelia Paget set off in the late summer of 1906, accompanied by her friend Mabel Ferguson of the Post Office who was to act as private secretary. After arriving by railway they travelled by horse and buggy about 1,100 miles, with Paget as the driver.[72] The two women camped out except when the weather was poor and then they stayed at the homes of Indian agents or farm instructors. In *The People of the Plains*, Paget expressed her admiration for the camping skills of the Plains people who "took the greatest possible comfort out of the camper's life, and had all its procedure reduced to a science… Anyone who had 'camped out' and travelled to any extent in the West before railways and stages had appeared would recall this resourcefulness and adaptability."[73] Paget did not require an interpreter except when speaking to the Assiniboine of Moose Mountain, and she visited there as well as the File Hills, Mucowpetung and Crooked Lake agencies. According to a Winnipeg newspaper report Paget interviewed the oldest inhabitants she could find and found it necessary to talk to a great many "to get all the facts." It was reported that she was cordially received as an old friend. Her method was to gather together several Elders and when one began to tell his or her narrative, the others would corroborate what was said, making corrections and adding further details. Certain stories were only told during the winter months, and Paget informed this reporter that she would need to return to record these, although she recalled many of them from her own childhood:

> The Indians have a series of such stories dating back to the flood; she used to hear them in her childhood and she is able to write many of them from memory: but it would be necessary for her to visit the people in the winter to get them to tell the old tales over again.

Among the notable persons she interviewed were the distinguished and aged Chief Piapot and Qui-witch, of the Sakimay Reserve, who was 102 years old. Paget expressed concern that she had little time, as the old people were rapidly passing and the younger generation was losing the elders' knowledge of earlier life. She believed that a number of visits would be necessary to complete her work, but it is unclear whether there were other visits. There was likely also a visit during the winter months, as the book features two chapters of "Wee-sack-ka-chack" stories, told only during the winter. According to Pullen-Burry, Paget returned in 1910, after the book was published, and travelled over 1,800 miles of prairies, "visiting the different reservations, where she is well known and where the Indians hailed her approach with feelings of genuine welcome. Here she read to various chiefs portions of her book, wherein she describes ceremonials, or folk-lore, asking them if she had given accurate descriptions."[74]

Paget submitted her manuscript to D.C. Scott who edited and reorganized the material. The extent to which he altered the work is unclear, but he may have rewritten some of it. E.S. Caswell, of Methodist Book and Publishing House and one of the readers of the manuscript, praised the material in a letter addressed to Scott, writing that "I don't think there is anything as good written on our Indians of the West."[75] He cautioned however that "Mrs. Paget has *the stuff* here, but fails in putting it into good literary form," and that it "will need to be practically rewritten." Caswell was "glad this work is in your [Scott's] hands, for I know it will be carefully done." It was Scott who corresponded with the publisher about the book's title, design, cover and illustrations. In the entire Department of Indian Affairs file dealing with the book there is no correspondence to or from Amelia Paget.

Some of Paget's ideas for the book were cast aside, apparently without any consultation with her. The title she had proposed for the book, in Cree or Saulteaux, was rejected. The publisher wrote "I shy at that musical but formidable title. It looks like a deliberate attempt to provoke lockjaw."[76] Painting and drawing by one of the McLean sisters was also rejected, as was Paget's idea for the cover ("I am returning under separate cover Mrs. Paget's original design."), and she appears to have had no say over the illustrations that were included, or their captions. The illustrations, which were collected by Scott and the publisher, were not always of the people featured in the book and they contain words Paget did not use such as "squaw." (An example is "Mutsinamakan and squaw, Sarcees," p. 2.) While it cannot be assumed with complete confidence, then, that *The People of the Plains* is entirely the work of Amelia Paget alone, it seems safe to conclude that the heart of the book, particularly her sympathetic and positive portrait, represents her own work, as Scott found it necessary to explain this approach in his introduction.

In the early days of their existence, Plains people were a "model race," according to Paget.[77] They had all they desired, including a nourishing diet and no sickness. They were hospitable, courteous, kind and generous. After describing modes of travel, how camping places were chosen and the tipis constructed, Paget depicted an idyllic scene:

> Such an encampment amid beautiful scenery, astir with prosperous and contented Indians, must have been a most striking illustration of the Indians' own idea of the wonderful love and care bestowed upon them by the Great Spirit... The young children played their games amidst these lovely scenes; the little babes, tied up in the mossbag or Indian cradle, awoke from their slumbers and looked upon the joyous and happy lives of their brothers and sisters, and grew up to appreciate everything which made life so pleasant an existence for their tribe.[78]

Paget argued that it was not "quite" fair to call Plains people pagans or heathens, and she provided extensive evidence of the depth and complexity of their religious beliefs.[79] She stressed especially their belief in the Great Spirit as the one Supreme Being, and clearly implied that this had a direct parallel to the Christian God:

> So in all their doings they never lost sight of the fact that for everything they must look to His help and love. And when the Indians were first met by intelligent white

Sketch by Sydney Hall, *The London Graphic*, December 17, 1881, p. 505

Buffalo dance at Fort Qu'Appelle, 1881, performed for the Governor General, Lord Lorne, and the vice-regal party. W.J. McLean organized and hosted the reception for Lord Lorne, and an estimated 1,400 Saulteaux and Cree gathered for the event. The McLeans were almost certainly in attendance, and this may be the dance which Amelia describes on pages 13–14.

> men, they certainly were examples of the blessings which come from faith in a higher beneficent Power.[80]

She wrote at length and in several places in the book about the powerful significance of dreams. Paget described many of their ceremonies and dances in great detail and she displayed a depth of understanding not found in other published accounts. An entire second chapter was devoted to the central religious ceremony of the Sun Dance, which as she explained is sometimes spoken of as the "Thirst Dance" among the Cree because in their language it was called "Nee-pah-quah-see-mun, which means 'dancing through a day and night without quenching one's thirst'."[81] Her description is unique, compared to other published accounts of that time which stressed the "barbarous" nature of the event with an emphasis only on the self-torture.[82] She described the complexity and deeper meaning of the Sun Dance as

> primarily a thank-offering to the Great Spirt, Kichie Manitou, for the re-awakening of all nature after the silence of the winter. It was a time for the making of braves, or, rather, an opportunity for the test of courage and endurance; it was a time for mourning their dead, and a time of petitions through their Pow-wah-kuns [dreams] for future blessings and love.[83]

While a ceremony like the Sun Dance was highly sacred and solemn, Paget also pointed out that other dances were intended for entertainment and to cause great merriment. At the "Giving-away Dance" many would "make up the most ridiculous words in praise of some article they were giving away, and thus cause no end of amusement to the onlookers."[84] The book contains many examples of Cree and Saulteaux humour including the practical jokes they delighted in playing on each other, such as the false alarm in the dead of night. No one was permitted to be vain and proud, as there were always "many wags who were ever ready to effect a cure for such cases."[85]

Derogatory representations of Aboriginal people are most directly challenged in Paget's treatment of women. As mentioned above, she did not use the term "squaw" at all in her text. She consulted women Elders in her fieldwork, writing that "One sometimes met with a particularly interesting old woman, whose life had been passed in keen observation of all the triumphs and trials of her band, who in a quiet and gentle manner would recount the many events she had lived through."[86] Women were featured throughout the book in a way that has remained rare until recent times. When writing about the Sun Dance Paget explained that women too went through certain forms of torture that "required a great deal of courage."[87] She noted that women and men took part in the Mee-tah-win or Medicine Dance but that women had their own special dances such as the Round Dance in which "they were very picturesque and graceful in their movements."[88] In describing the work of medicine men and women Paget had particular praise for the women specialists, whose cures of roots and herbs were in many cases wonderful.

Paget challenged the dominant stereotype of the "squaw drudge." The representation of the degraded position of the Indian woman, particularly as a beast of burden hauling wood behind her "lord and master" was a standard cliché.[89] Paget stressed that while they did carry the fuel and water, this was not a great hardship as they carried wood of the lightest kind and did not overburden themselves. Heavy logs were drawn by horses and young men chopped and cut the wood. "The popular idea of the poor Indian woman doing all the hard work has too often been overdrawn."[90] Another of the dominant stereotypes was of the enslavement of Plains women in polygamous marriage, and the notion that their lives were characterized by jealous bickering. Paget presented the practice of polygamy sympathetically, noting that the wives "called each other 'sister' and might, indeed, have been sisters in so far as their fondness for one another was concerned. They divided their labours equally, and tried in every way to cultivate mutual forbearance."[91] In many others ways Paget addressed misperceptions of Aboriginal women, demonstrating that they were excellent housekeepers, industrious workers and that they "displayed much artistic taste in their fancy-work. Their designs were perfect as to detail."[92]

Aboriginal women were described as the most attentive of mothers, challenging the sterotype of their indifferent and neglectful care that sustained the residential school system.[93] Paget wrote that "There surely never were any happier or healthier babies than the little Indian 'Awassisah'." Paget also stressed the bravery, courage and endurance of women. In describing warfare Paget wrote that "Many women, indeed, took part in these fights when the men were outnumbered, and by their daring and courage often turned the tide in their favour."[94] They were very modest, however, in speaking about their exploits. The insight Paget provides into the lives of Plains women is the most vivid example of the unique knowledge that she brought to bear to her project, and not just through her fieldwork but through her life experiences. Ethnographer David G. Mandelbaum, who in 1940 published his study regarded as the more definitive, scholarly work on the Plains Cree, did not have women informants, and his book lacks the rich detail on women found in *The People of the Plains*.[95]

Many of the prevailing representations of Plains people were directly confronted and challenged but in a muted, and understated tone. In her section on warfare she wrote that "The courage and daring of the Indians has often been discussed, and usually very much to their disadvantage..."[96] Their methods of warfare had been the subject of much disparagement in 1885, compared to representations of the heroic and dauntless Field Force.[97] But Paget "furnished evidence of the stuff the Indian was made of," stressing their "wonderful feats of bravery," as small expeditions could defeat "overwhelmingly larger numbers of the enemy..." In her section "Aboriginal Hospitality," Paget emphasized their kindness to strangers; they were not "of the savage nature so many writers have made them out to be..."[98] Her knowledge of the languages added great depth to these observations. She noted they had many phrases to express their hospitality:

> One of their favourite expressions when welcoming a stranger or a friend into their midst is "Ta-ta-wah," which means, "There is always room for you." Another expression when serving a visitor to a meal or any refreshment is "Kes-poo," meaning "May it satisfy you, or may it refresh you."

Paget carefully explained how certain practices that appeared cruel or heartless to outsiders, those condemned in the standard descriptions of Plains life, made sense in the Plains Cree and Saulteaux world. This is most obvious in her discussion of the Windigo complex. People who suffered dementia or who were insane were believed to be possessed by evil spirits and the greatest fear was that they would become cannibals. These people, if they did not recover through the intervention of medical specialists, were put to death. During the McLeans' months with the Cree in 1885 there was one such incident when an elderly woman named She-wins was killed because it was believed that she was dangerous to others. Paget explained that "The Indians, having no asylums or any means of isolating their unfortunate lunatics, were compelled to do away with them. It was utterly impossible for an Indian to go on a hunting expedition and leave his family to the mercy of a lunatic; so that any person showing marked signs of insanity was dispatched by his sorrowing and superstitious friends."[99]

The People of the Plains contains a wealth of information on the people and history of the Qu'Appelle Valley, with an emphasis on stories of deeds of bravery, courage and endurance. She recorded the story of the famous distance runner Acoose from the Sakimay Reserve, who, she wrote, in 1884 "ran after seven jumping deer" from Moose Mountain to the Crooked Lakes agency.[100] As mentioned above, one of Paget's main informants was Qui-witch, Acoose's father. One chapter is full of the histories of the "courageous dead, the great Koo-min-ah-koush, the intrepid Yellow-Head and the cunning Chim-ass-cous."[101] She provided deep understanding of how landscape features in the region of the Qu'Appelle came to have their names, writing that "the most appropriate place names in Canada are Indian names, and to assign to each and all their significance would be an attractive task."[102]

Paget's versions of these stories should not, however, be presumed to provide "authentic," "insider" perspectives, despite her background, knowledge of the languages, and longstanding acquaintance with the people she consulted. As Saulteaux historian Alex Wolfe relates in *Earth Elder Stories*, stories and songs belong to and are passed down through families, and the keepers and conveyors of these learn them over many years, not through brief visits.[103] Paget's understanding of Plains people was also filtered through prevailing ideas about a "vanishing race." Throughout the book there is a clear message that the Plains culture and way of life that Paget praised so highly had been significantly diminished and altered and that she is describing an ever-more distant past. This sentiment is expressed, for example, in her regret over the loss of dances, ceremonies and songs. Paget was passionate about Cree and Saulteaux music and the poetry of their words, and wrote that "It is a matter of regret that the Indians had no way of writing down or recording words and music. To many of them these are but a memory of happier times when upon every possible occasion they broke out into song. For them these times have gone, like the passing of the buffalo, never to return."[104] There were many other expressions of her belief that praiseworthy attributes were disappearing. Paget wrote, for example, of the "remarkable decline of good manners and polite usages among the Indians; years ago, everyone who studied their ways intimately was impressed with their dignity and fine manners."[105] Overall Paget appears to share the idea that prevailed in her time that Plains culture would vanish, and she sympathised with her Elder informants, "types of a dying race, in their lament for the days gone by when they were the sole inhabitants of the vast prairies in the West, free to roam wherever they felt inclined to go..."[106] Paget is also not able to entirely step outside of the detached observer status of an outsider of Euro-Canadian background. She describes certain customs and ceremonies as "peculiar" and some of their beliefs as superstitions.[107] Their faith in prayers she describes "as the faith of a little child."[108]

Yet *The People of the Plains* remains a remarkable and unique book in the social and cultural setting of the turn of the twentieth century. At that point the major published works on Western Canadian Aboriginal people were produced by missionaries who left the overall impression of a backward people inhabiting a world of ignorance, cruelty and superstition.[109] Missionaries stressed rather that a glorious future was in store for them if they cast aside their past and consented to be guided by their stronger and more enlightened guardians. Paget's book provided a sharp critique of these convictions and the shallow observations that characterized these books. She did not directly articulate her thoughts on the reasons for the decline she lamented but her book is a call for tolerance and generosity, hinting at a critique of government policy and parsimony. If she had more to say it would surely not have been wise to do so as her husband was employed by Indian Affairs and her project was sponsored by that department. Yet her message came through. She hints at a critique of the poor housing on the reserves that was a cause of tuberculosis and other diseases in her passage on the teepees of the past that were "comfortable and roomy, and could be kept fresh and clean; the opening at the top of the doorway caused a constant current of air, and they were very healthy places of abode."[110] In one of her most compelling passages that shows her understanding of Cree and Saulteaux Paget called for a greater sense of generosity:

> *Perhaps few realize how hard it is for our Indians to have to beg for the common necessities of life. They are naturally very proud and reserved, and among the older ones to beg is most humiliating. Being brought up to look upon everything as for the "common good," it is hard for them to have to remind people by begging that they are*

in want. There is, as a matter of fact, no such word in either the Cree or Saulteaux languages as "beg." The only thing approaching such a word in their language is "Puck-oo-she-twan" (Share with me). A nation whose expressive vocabulary holds no such words as "beg" or "beggar" we should be proud to help if ever it happens to be in need.[111]

Paget did her fieldwork and wrote at a time when activities such as the Sun Dance were banned under the Indian Act, when the mothering and housekeeping skills of women were criticized in government publications to justify the residential school system, and when distinguished chiefs were being deposed because of their beliefs and practices. She threatened powerful conventions and proposed a radical departure from prevailing wisdom.

Paget did not include herself and her experiences in *The People of the Plains* except for one brief passage at the end of her chapter on the Sun Dance when it is noted that it was regarded as an omen of misfortune and loss if a ceremony was disturbed by the approach of enemies and that "The last instance of such an unwelcome visit happened early in June 1885, during the North-West Rebellion. The Indians had only just begun the ceremonies when they were surprised by General Strange's column."[112] This is a curious addition that may have been inserted by D.C. Scott. Paget would have known from her fieldwork that Sun Dances were regularly being disrupted and broken up and the participants arrested, particularly under the administration of Scott, and she thus knew that 1885 was not the last incident of an unwelcome visit. It was Scott who provided details of Paget's background in his introduction to the book in which he felt it necessary to explain why Paget's portrait was so positive. He informed readers that the author and her family had been captured at Fort Pitt by Big Bear and his men and for a time had "shared all the hardships of his shifting camp." Scott claimed that it was this experience that accounted for her positive portrait of Plains people:

During this experience Mrs. Paget's knowledge of the Cree language and her intimacy with all the ways of the Indians, even the very fashion of their thoughts, proved a constant defence for the whole party. The following pages must be read by the light of these facts; they account for the tone of championship for all Indians, and for the idealistic tendency which places everything in a high and favourable aspect. If there were hardship, squalor, starvation, inhumanity and superstition in this aboriginal life, judged by European standards, here it is not evident.[113]

Scott suggested that both the author and her informants had overlooked the "real felicities of the situation" and that their memory of the events had been "heightened by the glow which might be spread over the reminiscences of some ancient chief whose lines had been cast in pleasant places, and to whom everything in the old days had become transfigured."

The People of the Plains elicited a variety of responses from reviewers.[114] There were positive reviews from those who appreciated the "first-hand information," were pleased to find that "her testimony tends to upset a number of popular superstitions," and who felt that the book ought to find a place in every library in the land.[115] The reviewer for the *Calgary Herald* wrote that "Mrs. Paget's book should be bought and read by everyone interested in the history and development of the Canadian West."[116] One reviewer appeared bemused that readers were to understand that wives agreed to polygamy, or that their language was poetic although they had no poetry.[117] Others were sharply critical such as the reviewer for the *Montreal Standard* who felt that the book contained too much "rose-color," that "even when free from contact with the white man they were not exactly the Arcadian shepherds and shepherdesses that Mrs. Paget presents ... the cruelty, the squalor, the dirt are glossed over. It is too late in the day for any Fenimore Cooper romance of the redskin."[118]

While her positive portrait was unpalatable to many readers, her work nonetheless had an important impact. It was read by artist Edmund Morris, quoted earlier, who painted portraits of Western Aboriginal people, including many mentioned in Paget's book. Like Paget, Morris was determined to preserve what he regarded as a vanishing Aboriginal past. (Two of his portraits appear in the book: one of Cree Chief Poundmaker, and another of the Chief Moonias, Ojibway.) In 1909 Morris was commissioned by the governments of Saskatchewan and Alberta to do portraits of Indians of those provinces and he received his copy of Paget's book during that trip.[119] (According to Morris biographer Jean S. McGill, one of his subjects, Blackfoot Medicine Man Wolf Collar, was a relative of Paget's.[120]) Although not heralded in his own time, Morris's work is regarded today as a vibrant, powerful record of the male leaders of the Plains people.[121]

The People of the Plains was of course read by Duncan Campbell Scott, and he would also have read any material that he edited out. He likely had conversations with Amelia Paget about the project as a whole including her informants. In his poem about Morris, who drowned in 1913, Scott borrows from Paget's book according to critic Leon Slonim.[122] In "Lines in Memory of Edmund Morris," set on the prairies, Scott imaginatively places himself and Morris inside the aged Saulteaux Chief Sakimay's tent to hear stories of the past. Scott was often "manipulating fact to serve the truth of the poem," and changed names and other features.[123] In this case Chief Sakimay could not have been his informant, as he had been dead since the 1880s, although a reserve in the Qu'Appelle Valley was named after him. It is also unlikely that Morris and Scott together had the occasion to be inside any Cree or Saulteaux Elder's tent as described.[124] It is likely that Scott based his portrayal of this ancient Elder on Paget's description of her meetings with Qui-witch, of the Sakimay reserve.

Amelia Paget did not continue to pursue a writing career after her book, although she did publish her report on a 1912 visit to Indian reserves for the Canadian Handicraft Guild.[125] She was a member of the Guild's Ottawa Branch. Participation in this organization permitted Paget to help preserve and revive Aboriginal traditions in a tangible way, and it also allowed her to pursue her critique, if muted, of government administration. This organization was opposed to the assimilation policies of the Department of Indian Affairs that sought to undermine Aboriginal fine arts and crafts.[126] The Guild, by contrast, was organized to "encourage, retain, revive and develop handicrafts and home art industries throughout the Dominion, and to prevent the loss and deterioration of these crafts."[127] In 1912 the Guild sent Amelia Paget to Saskatchewan to explain the organization's goal of reviving and perpetuating Aboriginal arts and crafts. She accompanied her father to James Bay and other northern areas covered by Treaty Nine, and then visited the reserves and schools of the people of her book in the Moose Mountain and Qu'Appelle districts. She found many women who excelled in beadwork, dressing leather and mocassin-making. She recommended to the Department of Indian Affairs that Indian handicrafts be taught at the Industrial School at Lebret, and she indicated in her report that an instructor was to be hired for that purpose. This report appears to have been Paget's last publication. She died in Ottawa on July 10, 1922 and is buried in the cemetery of old St. John's Cathedral church in Winnipeg along with many others of the old fur trade elite of the West.[128]

The fact that there were some appreciative reviews of Paget's book, and the work of the women of the Canadian Handicraft Guild, indicate that there were Canadians who were sympathetic to Paget's views and vision. But negative depictions resurfaced and prevailed. In 1910, the twenty-fifth anniversary of 1885, Western Canadian newspapers revived stories of "naked savages," and "horrible atrocities" committed during what were called the "Indian Massacres of 1885."[129] Edmund Morris responded to one such article entitled "Indian Savagery in the West," arguing that they were "in natural qualities ... far ahead of many of the whites with whom they are thrown in contact." Paget's response to such derogatory representations, that she would have been so keenly sensitive to during her lifetime, was eloquently expressed for all time in *The People of the Plains*. Like her contemporary, writer and performer E. Pauline Johnson, Paget "talked back," challenged demeaning narratives, and championed a more inclusive and tolerant nation, that would incorporate dignity and respect for Aboriginal people.[130] She did so, however, in a much more muted way, remaining the "cordial advocate."

I would like to thank the following for their assistance in bringing *The People of the Plains* back into print:

Edgar Mapletoft, Frenchman Butte
Brian Mlazgar, Canadian Plains Research Center, University of Regina
Anne Morton, Hudson's Bay Company Archives
Lally Grauer, Okanagan University College
Brenda Oslawsky, University of Calgary

Sarah Carter
Calgary, Alberta
September 2004

Notes

The text of Amelia Paget's book, and D.C. Scott's Introduction, have not been altered with the exception of changes to two captions for the illustrations where the word "squaw" has been removed. See the discussion of this issue above (p. xxi, note 60).

1. B. Pullen-Burry, *From Halifax to Vancouver* (Toronto: Bell and Cockburn, 1912), 122. It was noted on the title page of this book that Pullen-Burry was also the author of *Ethiopia in Exile, Jamaica As It Is*, and *A German Colony*.

2. Amelia M. Paget, *The People of the Plains* (Toronto: William Briggs, 1909). All further references and citations will be drawn from the new edition of this book (Regina: Canadian Plains Research Center, 2004).

3. Ann Laura Stoler, "Sexual Affronts and Racial Frontiers: European Identities and the Cultural Politics of Exclusion in Colonial Southeast Asia," in Frederick Cooper and Ann Laura Stoler (eds.), *Tensions of Empire: Colonial Cultures in a Bourgeois World* (Berkeley and Los Angeles: University of California Press, 1997), 198.

4. D.C. Scott, "Introduction," in Paget, *People of the Plains*, 14. Duncan Campbell Scott (1862–1947) spent 53 years as a civil servant in the Department of Indian Affairs, including 19 years in the top non-elected position of deputy superintendent general. He is better known, however, as a literary figure, a poet and essayist. See Brian Titley, *A Narrow Vision: Duncan Campbell Scott and the Administration of Indian Affairs in Canada* (Vancouver: University of British Columbia Press, 1986).

5. Paget, *People of the Plains*.

6. Sherry L. Smith, *Reimagining Indians: Native Americans Through Anglo Eyes, 1880–1940* (New York: Oxford University Press, 2000).

7. Ibid., 45.

8. Ibid., 5.

9. It was noted in the obituary for Amelia McLean's grandmother, Anne Campbell Murray, that she was born at Fort Dunvegan on Peace River in 1822 and that "She was the first white child to claim those distant northwestern regions as a birthplace. Her father being Colin Campbell, Chief Trader of the Hudson's Bay Company." Winnipeg, Manitoba Legislative Library, Manitoba History Scrapbooks, P1, p. 39. In Amelia's sister Kitty's memoirs a similar statement is made, although with more ambiguous wording. It was noted that Anne Campbell Murray "is said to have been the first white woman to enter the interior of northern Alaska, and her two daughters are said to be he first white children born there." Kitty McLean Yuill and Helen Yuill Perry, "Pioneers and Prisoners in the Canadian North West," 8 (unpublished, undated manuscript in the possession of Megan Wells of Winnipeg). Some exerpts were published as "Adventures of Kitty," in *The Nor'Wester* 100, no. 1 (July 15, 1970): 36–46.

10. National Archives of Canada (NA), Record Group (RG) 15, Department of the Interior, Series D-11-8-a, Volume 1322, Reel C-14931, scrip affidavit for Murray, Ann. Claim no. 1023; scrip no. 7762-7769; date of issue, July 30, 1876; amount $160.

11. NA, RG 15, Series D-11-8-a, Volume 1319, Reel C-14926, scrip affidavit for Campbell, Duncan. Claim no. 2217; scrip no. 11086; date of issue, October 2, 1876; amount $160; ibid., scrip affidavit for Bunn, Magdaline. Claim no. 2216, scrip no. 11085; date of issue October 2, 1876; amount $160; ibid., Volume 1322, Reel C-14931, scrip affidavit for Murray, Flora; ibid., scrip affidavit for McDonald, Eliza (née Murray); ibid., Volume 1319, Reel C-14925, scrip affidavit for Bedson, Jemima Mrs. (née Muray); concerning the claims of her five children.

12. Mary Fitz-Gibbon, *The Diaries of Edmund Montague Morris: Western Journeys, 1907–1910* (Toronto: Royal Ontario Museum, 1985), 92.

13. For a discussion of the issue of "native," "indigenous" or "insider" perspectives, see Kirin Narayan, "How Native is a 'Native' Anthropologist?" in Reina Lewis and Sara Mills, *Feminist and Postcolonial Theory* (New York: Routledge, 2003), 285–305.

14. In the *Manitoba Free Press* of July 11, 1922, it is noted that Amelia Paget was born at Fort Simpson.

15. http://www.fortsimpson.com/history.html

16. Obituary notice of Mrs. Alex H. Murray, Manitoba Legislative Library, Manitoba History Scrapbooks, P1, p. 39.

17. Marianne McLean, "John McGillivray," *Dictionary of Canadian Biography*, Vol. VIII (Toronto: University of Toronto Press), 546. See also Jennifer S.H. Brown, *Strangers in Blood: Fur Trade Company Families in Indian Country* (Vancouver: University of British Columbia Press, 1980), 98.

18. Simpson wrote "No. 64 McGillivray, Wm. A half breed of the Cree Nation. About 36 Years of Age 18 Years in the Service. Writes a good hand and rather clever, but of a Sour temper and a great deal of the sullen vindictive disposition of the Indian. Tyrranical and Oppressive in his management of the people by whom he is obeyed more through the fear of this Club than from personal respect. Manages the Trading Post entrusted to his charge very well. Conceited and self-sufficient like the generality of his Countrymen and altogether a disagreeable fellow. Has the vanity to look forward to an interest in the business but his prospects of success I imagine are very Slender. Stationed in New Caledonia District. (I have received information of his death since writing this.)" See "The 'Character Book' of Governor George Simpson, 1832," in Glyndwr Williams (ed.), *Hudson's Bay Miscellany, 1670–1870* (Winnipeg: Hudson's Bay Record Society, 1975), 222–23. Williams notes that Chief Factor William Connolly had a much higher opinion of William McGillivray, and thought he should have a much higher salary (p. 223).

19. Brown, *Strangers in Blood*, 181. See also Williams, *Hudson's Bay Miscellany*, 222–23.

20. Williams, *Hudson's Bay Miscellany*, 222–23.

21. McLean, "John McGillivray," 546. McGillivray and his second wife Isabella (McLean) lived on a farm near Williamstown, Upper Canada, and they had four sons and four daughters. Before his death in 1855 McGillivray returned briefly to Scotland to claim the estate of Dunmaglass and recognition as chief of the McGillivray clan. This recognition was officially awarded to his son (with Isabella) in 1857.

22. W.J. Healy, *Women of Red River: Being a Book Written from the Recollections of Women Surviving from the Red River Era* (Winnipeg: The Women's Canadian Club, 1923), 136.

23. Yuill and Perry, "Pioneers and Prisoners in the Canadian North West," 8.

24. Healy, *Women of Red River*, 169.

25. H.Y. Hind, *Narrative of the Canadian Red River Exploring Expedition of 1858*, Vol. 1 (1860; New York: Greenwood Press 1969), 340.

26. Liz Bryan, *The Buffalo People* (Edmonton: University of Alberta Press, 1991), 163.

27. Dan Ring (ed.), *Qu'Appelle: Tale of Two Valleys* (Saskatoon: Mendel Art Gallery, 2002), 36.

28. Quoted in ibid., 36.

29. Paget, *People of the Plains*, 163.

30. Isaac Cowie, *The Company of Adventurers: A Narrative of Seven Years in the Service of the Hudson's Bay Company During 1867–1874 on the Great Buffalo Plains* (Toronto: William Briggs, 1913), 465.

31. Ibid., 214–15.

32. W.A. Griesbach, *I Remember* (Toronto: The Ryerson Press, 1946), 31.

33. Yuill and Perry, "Pioneers and Prisoners in the Canadian North West."

34. Ibid., 29.

35. Ibid., 19.

36. Ibid., 20.

37. Ibid., 30.

38. Sarah Carter, *Lost Harvests: Prairie Indian Reserve Farmers and Government Policy* (Montreal: McGill-Queen's Press, 1990), chapter 2, "The 'Queen's Bounty'," 50–78.

39. N.M.W.J. McKenzie, *The Men of the Hudson's Bay Company* (Fort William: Times-Journal Presses, 1921), 62–63.

40. NA, RG 10, Records relating to Indian Affairs, Vol. 3687, File 13,698, F.L. Hunt to Edgar Dewdney, March 16, 1880.

41. Provincial Archives of Manitoba (PAM), MG 10 B6, St. John's College Ladies School Register of Attendance, Conduct and Marks, 1881.

42. Yuill and Perry, "Pioneers and Prisoners in the Canadian North West," 8.

43. Elizabeth M. McLean, "The Siege of Fort Pitt," *Beaver* Outfit 277 (December 1946): 22.

44. Sarah Carter, *Capturing Women: The Manipulation of Cultural Imagery in Canada's Prairie West* (Montreal: McGill-Queen's University Press, 1997), 51–60.

45. Sarah Carter, "Two Months in Big Bear's Camp, 1885: Narratives of 'Indian Captivity' and the Articulation of 'Race' and Gender Hierarchies in Western Canada," in R.D. Francis and Donald Smith (eds.), *Readings in Canadian History: Post-Confederation* (Toronto: Nelson Thomson Learning, 2002), 82.

46. Duncan McLean with Eric Wells, published as "The Last Hostage," in Harold Fryer (ed.), *Frog Lake Massacre* (Surrey, BC: Frontier Books, 1984), 81–82.

47. Charles R. Daoust, *Cent-vingt jours de service actif: Récit historique très complet de la campagne du 65ème au Nord-Ouest* (1886; English translation by Roberta Cummings: Wetaskiwin: City of Wetaskiwin, 1982), 58.

48. John D. Donkin, *Trooper in the Far North-West* (1889; Saskatoon: Western Producer Prairie Books, 1987), 158.

49. Charlottetown *Daily Patriot*, June 27, 1885.

50. Montreal *Daily Star*, June 23, 1885.

51. City of Edmonton Archives, W.J. Carter manuscript (unpublished), 1920, 56.

52. Anne Mercier and Violet Watt, *The Red House by the Rockies: A Tale of Riel's Rebellion* (London: Society for Promoting Christian Knowledge, 1896), 62.

53. Sylvia Van Kirk, "What if Mama is an Indian?": The Cultural Ambivalence of the Alexander Ross Family," 134. In John Foster (ed.), *The Developing West: Essays on Canadian History in Honour of Lewis H. Thomas* (Edmonton: University of Alberta Press, 1983).

54. Ann Laura Stoler, "Cultivating Bourgeois Bodies and Racial Selves," 91. In Catherine Hall (ed.), *Cultures of Empire: A Reader* (New York: Routledge, 2000).

55. Peter O'Leary, *Travels and Experiences in Canada, the Red River Territory, and the United States* (London: John B. Day Printer and Publisher, 1877), 145.

56. See Carter, *Capturing Women*, and Sarah Carter, *Aboriginal People and Colonizers of Western Canada to 1900* (Toronto: University of Toronto Press, 1999), chapter 8, "Turning Point: 1885 and After," 150–75.

57. Stoler, "Sexual Affronts and Racial Frontiers," 198.

58. Mariana Valverde, *The Age of Light, Soap and Water: Moral Reform in English Canada 1885–1925* (Toronto: McClelland and Stewart, 1991). See also Cicely Devereux, "'And Let Them Wash Me from This Clanging World': Hugh and Ion, 'The Last Best West' and Purity Discourse in 1885," *Journal of Canadian Studies* 32, no. 2 (Summer 1997): 100–115.

59. M. L'Abbé G. Dugast, "The First Canadian Women in the Northwest," in *Transactions of the Historical and Scientific Society of Manitoba* (Winnipeg: Manitoba Free Press, 1902), 62.

60. Quoted in Donna McDonald, *Lord Strathcona: A Biography of Donald Alexander Smith* (Toronto: Dundurn Press, 1996), 448. Minto's remarks here are curious in light of the fact that his own wife claimed to have Aboriginal ancestry. Mary, Countess of Minto, told the Kainai (Blood) of southern Alberta during an 1899 visit that she was descended from Indian "princess" Pocahontas. According to a policeman who accompanied the vice-regal party, "They were not at all impressed by the circumstances, and as a matter of fact, they did not believe the story." See R. Burton Deane, *Mounted Police Life in Canada: A Record of Thirty-one Years' Service* (London: Cassell and Co., 1916), 89.

61. Gerald Lynch, "An Endless Flow: D.C. Scott's Indian Poems," *Studies in Canadian Literature* 7, no. 1 (1982).

62. Veronica Strong-Boag and Carole Gerson, *Paddling Her Own Canoe: The Times and Texts of E. Pauline Johnson (Tekahionwake)* (Toronto: University of Toronto Press, 2000), 26.

63. E.K. Brown quoted in Stan Dragland, *Floating Voice: Duncan Campbell Scott and the Literature of Treaty 9* (Concord: Anansi, 1994), 191.

64. Ibid., 196.

65. *Ottawa Free Press*, July 11, 1922.

66. D.C. Scott, "Introduction," xxxvii, in Paget, *People of the Plains*.

67. *Regina Leader Post*, June 15, 1944.

68. NA, RG 10, Volume 4041, File 334503, Reel C-10178, "Report of F.H. Paget, who deals with the Western accounts, of his visit to Indian reserves and schools in Saskatchewan and Alberta, 1908."

69. D.C. Scott, "Introduction," xxxvii, in Paget, *People of the Plains*.

70. Manitoba Legislative Library, Manitoba History Scrapbook P1, 53. There is no date on the clipping and no newspaper source.

71. NA, RG 10, Volume 4018, Earl Grey to Frank Oliver, April 8, 1909.

72. The most extensive coverage of this trip is found in an article in the *Calgary Herald*, October 23, 1906. The rest of this paragraph is taken from this article.

73. Paget, *People of the Plains*, 29.

74. Pullen-Burry, *From Halifax to Vancouver*, 122.

75. NA, RG 10, Volume 4018, File 276,916, E.W. Caswell to D.C. Scott, January 8, 1909.

76. Ibid., Caswell to Scott, March 3, 1909.

77. Paget, *People of the Plains*, 2.

78. Ibid., 32. For an excellent and very different analysis of Paget's book see Shelly Hulan, "Amelia Paget's *The People of the Plains*: Imperialist and Ethnocritical Nostalgia," *Journal of Canadian Studies* 37, no. 2 (Summer 2002): 47–68.

79. Paget, *People of the Plains*, 1.

80. Ibid., 3.

81. Ibid., 5.

82. W.H. Withrow, *The Native Races of North America* (Toronto: Methodist Mission Rooms, 1895), 107–10.

83. Paget, *People of the Plains*, 5.

84. Ibid., 14.

85. Ibid., 45.

86. Ibid., 32.

87. Ibid., 8–9.

88. Ibid., 14.

89. Carter, *Capturing Women*, 109.

90. Paget, *People of the Plains*, 31.

91. Ibid., 40.

92. Ibid., 32.

93. Sarah Carter, "Categories and Terrains of Exclusion: Constructing the 'Indian Woman' in the Early Settlement Era in Western Canada," *Great Plains Quarterly* 13, no. 3 (Summer 1993): 150.

94. Ibid., 88–89.

95. David G. Mandelbaum, *The Plains Cree: An Ethnographic, Historical and Comparative Study* (1940; Regina: Canadian Plains Research Center, 1979).

96. Paget, *People of the Plains*, 25.

97. See, for example, the *Qu'Appelle Vidette*, December 10, 1885: "Indian warfare being a war of extermination without mercy to defenceless people, women and children."

98. Paget, *People of the Plains*, 43.

99. Ibid., 16.

100. Ibid., 27. There is much debate about this event. According to HBC employee N.M.W.J. McKenzie, the event took place in November 1886. His article in the *Qu'Appelle Vidette*, of December 2, 1886, was written on November 17, 1886, and he is describing an event that had just happened. According to McKenzie, Acoose chased a herd of elk or red deer on horseback from Moose Mountain to the Crooked Lake agency but there his horse played out and Acoose then started after them on foot, after obtaining ammunition from the HBC store there. He took off "like a streak of light passing over the snow" and within two hours shot three of the elk within three miles of the agency. McKenzie regarded this as an amazing feat and concluded that "Akoose [*sic*] should get a medal." In his diary Edmund Morris wrote that Paget was wrong in referring to them as deer and that they were elk, yet he called them deer himself in the catalogue to his 1909 exhibition that included his portrait of Acoose. See Stan Dragland, *Floating Voice: Duncan Campbell Scott and the Literature of Treaty 9* (Concord: House of Anansi Press Limited, 1994), 212. In his poem, "Lines In Memory of Edmund Morris," D.C. Scott writes that Acoose chased antelope (the "jumping deer that Paget refers to). According to Brenda Zeman, "anybody on Sakimay could have told him [Scott] it wasn't antelope, it was elk." Brenda Zeman, *To Run With Longoat: Twelve Stories of Indian Athletes in Canada* (Edmonton: GMS2 Ventures, Inc., 1988), 217.

101. Paget, *People of the Plains*, 27.

102. Ibid., 36. It is interesting to note that Duncan Campbell Scott's poem, "Indian Place Names," is about the traces of the past that linger in place names, beginning "The race has waned and left but tales of ghosts,/That hover in the world like fading smoke." See Duncan Campbell Scott, *The Poems of Duncan Campbell Scott* (Toronto: McClelland and Stewart, 1926), 22.

103. Alexander Wolfe, *Earth Elder Stories: The Pinayzitt Path* (Saskatoon: Fifth House, 1988), xi–xxii.

104. Paget, *People of the Plains*, 56.

105. Ibid., 44.

106. Ibid., 22.

107. Ibid., 2–3, 13.

108. Ibid., 1.

109. Sarah Carter, "The Missionaries' Indian: The Publications of John McDougall, John Maclean and Egerton Ryerson Young," *Prairie Forum* 9, no. 1 (Spring 1984): 27–44.

110. Paget, *People of the Plains*, 31.

111. Ibid., 44.

112. Ibid., 9.

113. D.C. Scott, "Introduction," xxxvii, in Paget, *People of the Plains*.

114. The book reviews are included in NA, RG 10, Volume 4018, File 276,916.

115. *Manitoba Free Press*, September 21, 1908, in NA, RG 10, Volume 4018, File 276,916.

116. *Calgary Herald*, August 21, 1909, in ibid.

117. *Ottawa Citizen*, August 29, 1909, in ibid.

118. *Montreal Standard*, October 9, 1909, in ibid.

119. Fitz-Gibbon, *Diaries of Edmund Montague Morris*, 92.

120. Jean S. McGill, *Edmund Morris: Frontier Artist* (Toronto and Charlottetown: Dundurn Press, 1984), 116. No reference is given for the statement: "Wolf Collar, a relative of Alexander McLean and Mrs. Paget, came to the camp to be painted." One possibility of a family connection is provided in the Fort Edmonton journal for 1826 when Chief Factor Rowand sent William McGillivray to live with the Peigan to halt the advance of American traders from the south. This

may have been Paget's great-great uncle, William McGillivray. For the information from the Fort Edmonton journal, see www.telusplanet.net/public/dgavneau/alberta2a.htm.

121. Geoffrey Simmins and Michael Parke-Taylor, *Edmund Morris "Kyaiyii" 1871–1913* (Regina: Norman Mackenzie Art Gallery, 1984).

122. Leon Slonim, "Notes on Duncan Campbell Scott's 'Lines in Memory of Edmund Morris." See http://www.uwo.ca/english/canadianpoetry/cpjrn/vol02/slonim.htm.

123. Dragland, *Floating Voice*, 209.

124. Ibid., 210. As Dragland notes, "there is no written evidence that Scott and Morris ever sat down together in Sakimay's tent, with the kinnikinnick and the stories." Dragland further notes, drawing on Morris's diary, that Morris did meet Scott and his wife in Regina, around July 25, 1910, while Scott was on a tour of inspection of the reserves. Scott then left for Duck Lake and File Hills. On August 10, 1910, Morris met Scott again at Lebret and the next day he accompanied Scott and Indian agent W.M. Graham to the Standing Buffalo Lakota reserve.

125. Amelia Paget, "Report on Mrs. Paget's Trip to Indian Reserves in Saskatchewan, 1912," in *Annual Report of the Canadian Handicraft Guild* (Montreal: Canadian Handicraft Guild, 1912).

126. Gerald R. McMaster, "Tenuous Lines of Descent: Indian Arts and Crafts of the Reservation Period," *Canadian Journal of Native Studies* 9, no. 2 (1989): 205–36. See also Ellen Easton McLeod, *In Good Hands: The Women of the Canadian Handicraft Guild* (Montreal and Kingston: McGill-Queen's University Press, 1999).

127. Quoted in McMaster, "Tenuous Lines of Descent," 211.

128. The inscription on her memorial stone reads:

Paget
Amelia McLean
Wife of F.H. Paget
Born July 16, 1867
Died July 10, 1922
To live in the hearts of those
we leave behind is not to die
"In thy light shall we see light." (Ps. 36.9)

Thanks to Shirley Collicutt, Office Manager, St. John's Cathedral, Winnipeg.

129. A series of articles appeared in the *Manitoba Free Press*, beginning April 1910, by John Hooper, who had been with General Middleton's column.

130. Strong-Boag and Gerson, *Paddling Her Own Canoe*.

Introduction to the 1909 Edition
by Duncan Campbell Scott

THERE ARE AT THE PRESENT TIME SEVERAL OLD INDIANS who believe that their fore-fathers, many years ago, came to this from some other continent; that they crossed a large body of water, landing at several different islands on their voyage; that they travelled towards the rising sun, and were stopped in their journey by unfriendly tribes. These hostile Indians forced them to settle upon the prairies, where they have dwelt for hundreds of years. A different language was spoken by their forefathers, and the country they came from was warmer than this part of the world.

They insist that the Great Spirit had guided them to this land, and had given it to them, with all its vast expanses teeming with game, from which they derived their sustenance. While they were the sole inhabitants of these territories they were wealthy; they had everything they could desire for their happiness, and they were proud of being what they were—the children of Kichie Manitou. When the white men came misfortunes came with them.

These ideas are mere shadows of dreams, the remnants of legends referring to migrations which are recent compared with the incalculable age of the race. The earliest explorers found established languages, tribes firmly fixed in their traditional territories, formalized manners and habits. But ages upon ages had passed in which the form of the continent had changed, and again changed, before these peoples had become differentiated. Where was the cradle of the race; drifting from what plateau or valley came the progenitors of the tribes who were in possession when the Northmen and Columbus first touched the shore? The answer to the question takes the form of conjecture and suggestion, but investigation of this interesting ethnological problem has proceeded so far that all the unscientific theories of the last hundred years have been abandoned and a working hypothesis established which may be varied, modified or strengthened, but which, a hundred years from this, may have been firmly established by evidence which is not now available. The theory that they were the descendants of the "ten lost tribes" of Israel has had its day, and that which traces their coming to an easterly migration by way of Behring Straits or the Aleutian Islands is slowly passing.

As these preliminary words are only intended to serve the purpose of connecting the Indian of to-day with some past, even the indefinite and speculative, instead of leaving him without any affiliation with the general human stock, it will not be advisable to give any extended argument cogent to the theory of such affiliation, but simply to state the theory itself.

The explanation which gains force from geological and other scientific evidence is that the inhabitants of this continent cane from Europe by a westerly migration across a huge land bridge which gave continuous communication in an equable climate by way of Iceland and Greenland. The subsidence of this plateau, which now forms the shallow bottom of the North Atlantic, cut off the people of our continent from other portions of the world, and left them to develop amid the circumstances and environment which evolved during the succeeding ages.

Anyone more than superficially interested in this fascinating subject may begin his reading with the last chapter of Frederick S. Dellenbaugh's "The North Americans of Yesterday." He may then be tempted to read Dr. David G. Brinton's "The American Race," where he will find a condensed but exhaustive treatment of the matter.

There is no doubt that the native inhabitants of North America are of one race, with strongly marked characteristics, but with many linguistic variations and other less important tribal distinctions arising from environment. Chief among the linguistic stocks is the Algonquin, which extends over a larger area than any other. From as far north as the Peace River and the Churchill River to North Carolina, and from the Atlantic coast to the Rocky Mountains, the tribes of this great division possessed the land. They now number about ninety-five thousand, and the main tribal divisions are as follows: Abenakis, Algonquin, Blackfoot, Cree, Mississauga, Micmac, Ojibway and Ottawa.

The four tribes inhabiting the Provinces of Saskatchewan and Manitoba, which are described in the succeeding chapters, are the Crees, Saulteaux (a name given to the Ojibways by the early French explorers, who first found them at Sault Ste. Marie), Assiniboines and Sioux. Of these four tribes the Crees and Assiniboines were the first inhabitants of the provinces.

The Crees are to be found from the shores of Hudson Bay to the foot of the Rocky Mountains, and as far north as the Beaver River, and even farther north. They claim that they were the original owners of the vast prairies of the western provinces, and that eventually the tribe was joined by the Assiniboines, who are a branch of the Dakota stock.

The Sioux, another branch of the Dakota stock, who now form part of our Indian population, are refugees from south of the international boundary. These Indians in times long past were the sworn enemies of the Crees and Saulteaux, and would follow them, especially the former, into their own territory often as far north as the Saskatchewan River. In later years they came into Canada, fleeing from justice, taking refuge in Manitoba and Saskatchewan. They were responsible for many outrages upon the early pioneers in Minnesota and Dakota, but have been peaceable and law-abiding since they became wards of the Dominion. They come of the once powerful Dakota stock, and are fine specimens of the Indian race.

The Ojibways, another large branch of the great Algonquin stock, occupy the vast area between Hudson Bay and James Bay on the north and Lakes Superior and Huron on the south.

It seemed necessary to write these few words upon the probable origin of the Indians and upon the tribes specially dealt with in the following pages, so that the reader might not find himself, without introduction, in the very midst of the subject.

Moreover, books dealing with Indian manners and customs have not been so frequent of late that a new one may pass without comment, and the present volum. has special claim to more than momentary attention by reason of its authentic value. It is the easiest of easy tasks, at this day, to compile a volume about anything; stated facts are common property, be they or be they not trustworthy, and with a little industry and a certain amount of literary craftsmanship, any person may patch up a book about Indians, a subject that does not lose its interest. But the present work is no compilation; it is a statement of personal experience, and has all the merit of orig- inal observation. One cannot deny to these pages the interest which flows from this source. No literary charm can condone for imperfect material, but often the author's knowledge of his subject lends a certain grace to his style; this latter claim may safe- ly be made for these unaffected chapters. Mrs. Frederick H. Paget, when her father, Mr. W. J. MacLean, was an officer of the Hudson's Bay Company, had many oppor- tunities to gain at first-hand the information which is now given to the public. Moreover, she was gifted with a language-sense which made possible a knowledge of the subtlest peculiarities of two languages, the Cree and Ojibway, both highly expres- sive, but the last eminently flexible and poetic. Thus from her earliest years she was brought into contact with the best specimens of the two races. Qu'Appelle, where her father was Factor for eight years, was a particularly favourable observation-point when that post was thronged with a free concourse of Indian and half-breed traders. The plains were furrowed by cart-tracks only, and dotted with the fugitive shelters of the aborigines; the buffalo was disappearing, and the time for change was upon them— yet still the Indian was lord of his domain. Active tribal warfare had ceased, but the post was alive with men who had been upon the warpath and whose lodges were dec- orated with the trophies of foray and ambush. The position which the Factor held gave his daughter, no doubt, special privilege and opportunity; and growing skill in the language added the last power to win the confidence of these proud, shy people. And two years after, during the half-breed troubles of 1885, Miss MacLean with her father and the rest of his family had sharp experience of the trials which attend upon Indian hostilities. Captured at Fort Pitt in April of that year by Big Bear and his braves, they were held until the 17th of June following, sharing all the hardships of his shifting camp. During this experience Mrs. Paget's knowledge of the Cree language and her intimacy with all the ways of the Indians, even the very fashion of their thoughts, proved a constant defence for the whole party. The following pages must be read by the light of these facts; they account for the tone of championship for all Indians, and for the idealistic tendency which places everything in a high and favorable aspect.

If there were hardship and squalor, starvation, inhumanity and superstition in this aboriginal life, judged by European standards, here it is not evident. All things are judged by the Indian idea of happiness, and the sophistication of the westerner dis- appears. The real felicities of the situation are heightened by the glow which might be spread over the reminiscences of some ancient chief whose lines had been cast in pleasant places, and to whom everything in the old days had become transfigured. This animating spirit is pleasant; there is no reason why the arrogance of our so-called civilization should everywhere prevail, and it is probably fortunate that, when the Dominion Government set apart a small appropriation for the purpose of gleaning such memories as remain of the bygone domestic life of the western tribes, the task should have fallen to the lot of one whose early training placed her rather in the seat of the cordial advocate than in that of the frigid critic.

he picture here presented is not complete in every detail, yet when the
ers and customs of the Crees and Saulteaux have changed and become
r of conjecture or of vague recollection, this book will be sought as a
of many old things that have passed away.

Duncan Campbell Scott
Department of Indian Affairs.
April, 1909

Chapter 1

• A primeval faith • Kichie Manitou • Machie Manitou • Pow-wah-kunah • The Happy Hunting Ground • Burial customs • Trust in the Great Spirit.

"The Indians of North America, as I have before said, are copper-coloured, with long, black hair, black eyes, tall, straight and elastic forms—are less than two millions in number—were originally the undisputed owners of the soil, and got their title to the land from the Great Spirit, who created them on it—were once a happy and flourishing people, enjoying all the comforts and luxuries of life which they knew of, and consequently cared for—were sixteen millions in number, and sent that number of daily prayers to the Almighty, and thanks for His goodness and protection."**

T HE FOREGOING IS QUOTED FROM ONE OF CATLIN'S LETTERS. As he was one of the first white men who travelled among the Indians to study their habits and characteristics, spending eight years among them (1832-1839), it is worthy of note that he found them offering prayers to the Great Spirit. And their faith in these prayers was as the faith of a little child; so that in speaking of the Indians it is not quite fair to call them pagans or heathens. Their belief in the Great Spirit (Kichie Manitou) as the one Supreme Being who held their destiny in His keeping, and whom they worshipped indirectly through the thunder, the wind and other manifestations of nature, places them above such a soulless classification. They also believed in the Bad Spirit (Machie Manitou), who was felt to be near them, ever tempting them to stray into paths of wickedness, and whom they believed to be responsible for all harm and affliction which befell them.

They would never worship the Great Spirit directly, counting themselves unworthy to address Him, but through some of His works. Thus one Indian would ever plead through the thunder for such blessings and gifts as he desired, another would approach Him through the winds, or through the lightning, or through some bird or animal. Their faith in their intercessors was remarkable.

Certain members of the tribe were believed to have closer communion with their particular intermediator, and these gifted Indians possessed wonderful second sight; they were consulted in times of pressing necessity and urged to plead for blessings or guidance.

These intermediators were called Pow-wah-kunah (meaning dreams), and every confidence was placed in them. They had a wonderful significance for each Indian,

---

* Catlin's *North American Indian*, Vol. 1, page 6.

Mutsinamakan and wife, Sarcees (for a discussion of the caption, see page xxi and xxii).

practically influencing every action of his life. Nothing would be undertaken until the Pow-wah-kun was appealed to, so that the blessing of the Kichie Manitou might fall upon such effort.

The Indians' idea of the life beyond the close of the one spent here is certainly worth to them any amount of hardship and suffering. They believe that after death a few days or weeks (according to the lives they led upon this earth) shall find them at their journey's end, and in a land teeming with game of all kinds, where they shall live a perfect life forever and ever. This land is called the Happy Hunting Grounds, a land which must indeed be worth attainng if the pictures they dream of it have any-where any realization in fact. All Indians, according to their belief, will reach this land in the end. Some will take longer than others on the journey, as on the way they will meet with hardships and difficulties in order to atone for sins committed on this earth.

In the early days of their existence in this territory, they were a model race. Their misdeeds were very few, and they were honourable to a degree. But if anyone trans-gressed and committed some trivial wrong or misdemeanor, he or she realized that the journey to the future home would be made more difficult by the Good Spirit. And to help these less fortunate ones, their friends on earth would provide them, for weeks and months after their departure, with provisions, wearing apparel, weapons and utensils for their use during the journey to the Happy Hunting Grounds.

It was customary for the Indians to dispose of their dead upon scaffolds. These were built of four good, stout poles of from ten to twelve feet in length, stuck firm-ly in the ground, and on the top of these would rest other poles, making a stage of the desired size. And on this peculiar construction would be placed the dead body, wrapped in many rolls of finely dressed buffalo or deer skins. With the body would be placed the dead Indian's most treasured possessions—in the case of a brave, his pipe and weapons, and the scalps of any enemies he had been fortunate enough to take in time of war, together with his festive garments and two or three pairs of moccasins. Near the scaffold would be left any other articles which his friends considered necessary for his use on the journey across the valley which divides this earth from the Happy Hunting Grounds.

It was considered a good omen if rain fell shortly after the burial of the departed. The body was placed on the scaffold so that the rain falling down from the heavens (Kichie-kisek-kouck, great and good skies) upon the dead body would cleanse it of all its sins and hasten its arrival at the Happy Hunting Grounds. This was their belief as to the washing away of their sins.

The Indian, in speaking of any incident in his life, would always emphasize the fact that he was loved by the Great Spirit, or Kichie Manitou; for example, he might relate the incidents of some very hard journey he had successfully undertaken, and would conclude the narrative by saying that it was accomplished because of the great love of the Kichie Manitou. They never imagined themselves capable of doing even an unimportant thing without this love which they believed in so firmly.

If any member of their tribe or any friend were leaving for some long journey, or for even a few days, they would always say, "May the love of the Great Spirit be with you."

In time of war, when hard pressed by the enemy, some members of their band would always encourage them to greater effort by reminding them of this great love. If they were the victors, they would be reminded that the victory was theirs only through this love. If they met with defeat, it was because they had not trusted sufficiently in the love of the Great Spirit. So in all their doings they never lost sight of the fact that for everything they must look to His help and love. And when the Indians were first met by intelligent white men, they certainly were examples of the blessings which come from faith in a higher beneficent Power.

Chapter 2

*• The Sun Dance • The invitation • The search for the centre pole • Building the
lodge • Enter the dancers • The making of braves • Forms of torture.*

THE PRINCIPAL RELIGIOUS CEREMONY OF THE CREES was undoubtedly the Sun
Dance, sometimes spoken of as the Thirst Dance. In the Cree language it was
called Nee-pah-quah-see-mun, which means "dancing through a day and night without quenching one's thirst."

Passionately attached as are the Crees to this ceremony, it is evidently foreign to
the Algonquin stock. While religious beliefs are common to all the tribes of this great
family and are persistent everywhere, this extraordinary religious function is known
only to the Blackfeet, the Western Crees and the Dakotas. The Ojibways do not
practise it, and there are no traces of it among the eastern divisions of the race.

This ceremony only took place in the early summer, generally in the month of
June, the moon of Young Birds,* and was primarily a thank-offering to the Great
Spirit, Kichie Manitou, for the reawakening of all nature after the silence of winter.
It was a time for the making of braves, or, rather, an opportunity for the test of
courage and endurance; it was a time for mourning their dead, and a time of peti-
tions through their Pow-wah-kuns for future blessings and love.

Those taking part in it did so at the invitation of the Indian who felt himself worthy to give such a great ceremony. And this Indian would not send out his invitations

---

* The authority for the following names for months (moons) of the year is the old Indian, Qui-
witch, who is referred to on page 27:
The first moon.
The eagle moon.
The goose moon.
The frog moon.
The mating moon.
The egg moon.
The young birds' moon.
The moulting of birds moon.
The young birds fly moon.
The shedding of horns moon.
The falling leaves moon.
The falling snow moon.
The hard ice moon.

Chief Moonias, Ojibway, by Edmund Morris.

on the impulse of the moment, but would give the subject long and serious consideration. The information as to who intended giving the Nee-pah-quah-see-mun was usually made known early in the winter. This was done in order to avoid any confusion which might arise if another member of the band had thought of issuing invitations for such a ceremony.

The invitations were sent by trusty messengers, usually picked from the younger men of the band, and to them was entrusted the pipe of peace. This pipe might well be called a "pipe of ceremony" too, as it played an important part in all such events. The messengers would ride to distant friendly bands, and convey to them the information that they carried the pipe from a certain member of their band, who extended to them an invitation to take part in the Nee-pah-quah-see-mun. After the acceptance of the invitation by the smoking of the pipe, the messengers would go on to some other band. The invitation was usually conveyed in the following words: "We are young men from (say) Day Star's band, and bring an invitation to you from White Bear, one of our headmen, who requests you to take part in the Nee-pah-quah-see-mun which he is arranging for the second week in the month of young birds (June) at the Last Stand Hill. It is to be a time of thank-offering to the Kichie Manitou for all His blessings to us during the past winter and for the return of summer, with all its promises of plenty. Come in time to help erect the lodge in which it is to take place."

Very few, if any, Indians did not avail themselves of this invitation. And a few days before the time appointed, many wigwams would be added to those of the band already assembled at the place mentioned. This spot was usually chosen for its beauty, and was generally situated on some hill or mountain-side, with timber and water in abundance.

When all the Indians who had accepted the invitation had arrived, the most imposing part of the ceremony was begun. This was the search for and finding of a suitable poplar tree for the centre of the dancing lodge. A large number of the braves of the tribe, dressed and painted in festive attire, all mounted upon their best horses, and carrying guns and rifles, would ride off in search of a huge poplar tree. When a decision was reached as to the finest tree found, they would fire off round after round of ammunition, and proceed to cut down the tree. After this was accomplished, the Indians would fasten cords or ropes, made of buffalo skin, around the end and lower branches of the tree, and again mounting, would haul it to the spot upon which the lodge was to be built. During the ride they would sing a special song, and fire off numerous volleys from their rifles and guns. This singing and firing was kept up until the tree, shorn of all its lower branches, was placed in position. It occupied the exact centre of the lodge, and was usually firmly planted in the ground at a depth of three or four feet. The rest of the lodge was also built of poplar poles or posts, all green, as no dry or decayed wood was allowed to be used in its construction. These poles, which were ten or twelve feet in height, were planted in the ground around the central post, forming a large circle of about forty or fifty feet in diameter, leaving an opening on the south side of about thirty feet for an entrance. The roof was also made of poles covered over with the green branches of the trees. In the inside fully half, or even three-quarters, of the north side of the lodge was divided off into numerous small compartments by short posts set in the ground, with a lattice-work of rawhide thongs around each. All the spaces would be filled by a basket-work of green boughs; but in each cell or compartment was a small opening, just large enough to permit a person to crawl in. These openings were at the back of the cells facing the large space left in the lodge. Each compartment was just large enough to hold a person when in a sitting posture, and all were of a uniform height of, say, four and a half feet. Around the opening at the top of each ran a piece of rawhide thong to give strength to the structure, but this was usually hidden by the green leaves and branches forming the basket-work. This lodge or green bower, though very large, was built in a surprisingly short space of time by willing hands; all the builders being in high spirits during its construction.

When ready it would at once be filled by as many of the dancers as it could accommodate, each cell or compartment being occupied by an Indian brave or woman dressed in his or her best, with face painted in all the brilliant colours of the rainbow. As their entrance was made very quickly and secretly from the back of the lodge, the effect was startling to an onlooker, when the drumming and singing began, and all the dancers rose out of the mass of green foliage of which the cells were made. In the mouth of each dancer was held a small whistle or flute, made from the leg-bone of the crane. These little pipes were gaily decorated with streamers of coloured deer skin or ribbon, coloured porcupine quills and beads, but never heavily ornamented, as they were to be held for so long a time in the mouth of each dancer. The dancing consisted of an up and down movement of the body without rising from the feet, to the rhythm of the drumming and chanting, and at each downward movement of the body the piping note from the little flute was blown by the dancer. All these soft little notes were wonderfully sweet, and seemed to harmonize with the chanting of the men and women who were the musicians for the occasion. These singers were relieved by others at short intervals, but the Indians taking part in the dance were expected to dance and fast for a day and a night (twenty-four hours) at the very least--though upon occasion some only danced for a short time, say, ten hours.

The ceremony usually lasted three or four days, according to the number wishing to take part in it. The dancers were expected to keep their eyes upon the central post during the time they danced, and this was done even when other Indians were going through all kinds of torture near the lodge.

The making of braves consisted of enduring all manner of self-inflicted tortures. Certain of these never varied; they were suffered by those who had previously qualified in other Nee-pah-quah-see-muns. Only a few Indians at each ceremony prepared for these degrees of torture.

The most trying of all these was the leading of a spirited horse right up to the central post of the lodge. The Indian going through this degree required any amount of courage and endurance, as the horse was led by a leather line or thong attached to two small sticks or skewers which had been stuck through the fleshy part of the Indian's body just over the shoulder-blades. These skewers were about five or six inches long, and fully two inches of the centre of each stick was imbedded in the flesh. Around the ends of each would be fastened a noose of the leather thong, and to these the longer or leading line was attached. The task of passing the sharp skewers through the flesh of the would-be brave was always performed by the medicine man.

The Indian leading the horse usually began the ordeal by making a wide circle around the encampment, and gradually lessening the distance as the horse became accustomed to the noises of the drumming and singing, until at last he would walk into the opening of the lodge or bower and right up to the central post. This was not an easy matter, as the horse would often refuse to go into the lodge, and even attempt to run away sometimes. At other times an Indian would be fortunate enough to have a spirited animal who would follow his master into any place, and not give him any unnecessary torture.

When once the Indian had walked up to the central post of the lodge, he was released from his torture by the medicine man, who pulled the sticks out of his back, at the same time remarking that his "heart was strong."

Another form of taking this degree of courage was by trailing upon the ground an old buffalo head by means of a leather thong fastened to the skewers or sticks through an Indian's back. This was also a very painful performance, as the horns of the buffalo head would often become entangled in brush or heavy grass, necessitating many painful stops and round-about ways in order to extricate the horns. The Indian would haul this head around the whole encampment, gradually working his way to the lodge, and after reaching the large post would be released. The Indians would sometimes faint while undergoing these peculiar ordeals to attain the envied degree of bravery. Those who got through without losing consciousness would very soon be seen in the cells dancing as if they had not undergone anything out of the ordinary. If they were pale from the effects of the torture the pallor was hidden by the extra amount of paint used on their faces when dressing for the dance.

Anyone not familiar with the features of the Indians taking part in the dance might not recognize them after each interval of dancing, as during the intermissions between the singing and dancing, in the seclusion of their cells, they would paint their faces in an entirely different style and colour.

The re-appearance of an Indian in the dance always created a flutter of excitement, and caused many flattering remarks as to his bravery and powers of endurance. But an Indian never boasted of these feats; and if he ever did refer to them, did so in a very casual and modest way. In any case it was most unlikely that any of the Indians who had seen him undergoing the torture would or could forget his courage—and they would speak of it for years after.

The women also underwent certain forms of torture, and these, too, required a great deal of courage. These self-sacrifices on the part of the women were, properly speaking, memorial offerings for their departed loved ones. The woman who wished to undergo this suffering had her arms from the elbow down slashed with cuts from a sharp knife; this was also done by the medicine man. In the case of the women the torture was inflicted after they had taken part in the dance. Some women, and men also, would have their hair cut short, as a memorial for their dead. As every Indian was proud of his hair, these offerings, though painless, required great self-sacrifice.

During the time the Sun Dance was in progress, any Indian taking part gave to the spirits of his departed friends, according to his means, offerings which were hung upon the trees or poles for three or more days, after which lapse of time they were taken away by friends of the donors if they wished to appropriate them. It was a real gift, as they never resumed them. In this interval of three or four days, it was held that the spirits had used them fully, and after that time they might be fairly taken and utilized by the living. These offerings are supposed to be required by the souls of the Indians in the Happy Hunting Grounds, and they were various—anything, in fact, from wearing apparel to cooking utensils, even steel traps, being offered. But these offerings were really unnecessary, as every Indian taking part in the ceremony could do so as a memorial service or as a thank-offering for the return of summer, or by way of petition to his Pow-wah-kun.

Sometimes these Nee-pah-quah-see-mun ceremonies were disturbed by the approach of enemies. At such a time they might easily be stolen upon, as all entered into the spirit of the performance so heartily that they were apt to forget the existence of any hostile tribes. They looked upon such surprises as an omen of misfortune and loss. The last instance of such an unwelcome visit happened early in June, 1885, during the North-West Rebellion. The Indians had only just begun the ceremonies when they were surprised by General Strange's column.

Chapter 3

THE FEAST SECOND IN IMPORTANCE WAS THE MEDICINE DANCE, or Dog Feast, called by the Indians the Mee-tah-win. This, also, took place during the summer season, as the lodge was made of green trees and branches. It was built in the shape of a long "A" tent, with an opening at either end. There were also several openings in the roof of the lodge to allow the escape of smoke from the fire which they built in the middle. The lodge was generally very large, fully thirty or forty feet in length, and high enough to permit the Indians to dance around the fire in its centre.

This feast was for the medicine men, and very few other Indians took part in it. Those who did so signified their intention of becoming medicine men, and were taught many of the arts of healing by the older members of the cult. For this tuition they had to pay very liberally. Women also were allowed to take part in this dance, and joined in learning the medicinal properties of herbs and roots.

The Indians, both men and women, who furnished the singing and drumming for the festival sat at one side of the fire, usually near one of the entrances, the drumming being always done by the men. The shrill voices of the women, pitched in a minor key, blended very effectively with the deeper tones of the men, and from a distance the sounds were very harmonious.

Each dancer would carry around small stuffed animals, such as the mink and weasel, fastened to long, slender sticks. During the dance around the fire they would thrust these little medicine-charms into the faces of the onlookers. If the dancer pointed the little token at one of the spectators (who gave every attention to the dance) that one immediately bowed the head, thus ensuring himself against any evil which might have emanated from the charm. It was supposed by the Indians that a hard substance would soon be felt in the throat, if the head was not bowed immediately. This substance would eventually cause death if allowed to remain in the body, and therefore it is easy to understand the attention given to every dancer.

Some of the dancers, who were known to be kind and friendly, very seldom indulged in this practice, but the older medicine men, and those who were stricter in their observances of the rules of the Mee-tah-win, followed closely this part of the ritual which might be attended by such fatal results.

At this ceremony or rite the medicine men would serve dog-flesh to any of the Indians who wished to partake of the dish. The dog was killed by being hanged, and

A chief and his family.

after it was quite dead would be singed, not skinned, and cooked over the fire in the medicine lodge. After it was cooked the medicine men would be served first, then the other Indians. It was considered a very great honour to eat dog with the medicine men at this feast, and every Indian who could be present would be served with a small portion.

After the feast, or Mee-tah-win, was over (it usually lasted four or five days), the Indians world give away or throw away all manner of things to their Pow-wah-kunah (dreams). These offerings would be hung from poles, trees, etc., and generally on some hill or elevation. They would consist of buffalo robes, red and blue cloth, blankets, prints or calicoes, moccasins and other wearing apparel, fire-arms, cooking utensils, etc. For days and even months these offerings would attract the eye of the traveller passing by the place where the Mee-tah-win had been held. If any one were curious enough to make a careful examination of the land in the vicinity they would find many offerings of Indian medicine hidden away in holes and under shrubs. This medicine was offered to the Great Spirit so that He would give to the person offering it more skill in the treatment of all ailments and greater knowledge of roots and herbs.

None of the Indians ever disturbed these gifts of medicine, as they were supposed to bring bad luck and misfortune to the person touching them. Sometimes this medicine was poison, and it was for the Bad Spirit, who in return for the offering was supposed to work all imaginable harm to the enemies of the medicine man or woman who left the poison as an offering.

The fact that these caches of medicine consisted sometimes of poisons may have been one reason why they were never disturbed; the Indians being terrified of "bad medicine," as its effect was usually most disfiguring, and all Indians (especially the men) are most vain of their personal appearance.

These two ceremonies had more significance for them than any other of their dances. Every one of the dances had a peculiar and special importance, and though all were to a certain extent a thanksgiving to the Great Spirit, none were so solemn and impressive as the Nee-pah-quah-see-mun (Sun Dance) and Mee-tah-win (Medicine Dance).

The Indians in the years long past had another ceremony which they called the "Smoke Dance." This was a festival in connection with the pipe of peace, the consecrating ceremony of a new pipe. It is many years now since such a dance was celebrated among our Indians, and very little is known of it.

The Indians taking part in it gave thanks to the Great Spirit for giving them the red sandstone for the making of their pipes, and for the red willow, of which the pipe stems were made. The dance was given by an Indian (or two or three Indians) who had been given the pipe of peace, generally in recognition of some act which called for an extra amount of bravery, or by those who had finished the tedious task of making the pipe. During the ceremony the pipes would be taken out of their wrappings of soft deerskin and fine furs, and after being filled with the dried inner bark of the red willow (which the Indians used when they had no tobacco, and which they still use with tobacco), they would light it with a live ember from the fire, and before placing it near the mouth, would point to the four principal points of the compass and to the heavens above and the earth underneath, then they would each inhale once from the pipe as it was passed around. After the pipe had been smoked by every Indian present the musicians would start their singing and drumming, and the dancing would begin; the owners of the pipe dancing around and pointing with the pipe and stem in the directions above-mentioned. Considering the significance to them of the pipe of peace, it would seem possible that this dance was looked upon by the Indians as being quite as important as the Medicine Dance or Dog Feast.

Many of their dances were indulged in after a battle, and these were in every way a thanksgiving to the Great Spirit for their deliverance from the hands of their enemies, but were of a joyful character. The War Dance was performed before a contemplated battle, the Scalp Dance after it had been fought and won.

The Buffalo Dance was a very peculiar one, and was indulged in by very few of the Indians. Those taking part in it would paint or colour all their bodies with red clay, and would wear a buffalo head or mask, which had been skinned and dried, with the horns complete, and which looked wonderfully natural; into their belts at the back they would stick the tail of a buffalo, and around their ankles they wore strips of buffalo hide. The very heaviest part of the fur, taken from the boss or hump, was used for these anklets. In their hands the dancers carried long spears, decorated with buffalo tails, and coloured strips of dressed buffalo-skin. The dancers were formed in a very large circle, but not confined to it, in the centre of which stood a young boy and girl, holding in their hands a small vessel containing some kind of medicine.

These children would be kept standing for hours at a time while the Indians danced around them; and as the dancers could sit down and rest between intervals of singing and drumming, they never seemed to realize how very tired the two youngsters could become, or if the day was very hot, how harmful it was for them. Upon the last celebration of this dance at Fort Qu'Appelle, the little girl fainted before the ceremony was finished.

The Indians taking part in it would jump up as soon as the musicians started their singing and drumming, and after running around all or part of the circle, would dance about as long as the music lasted; as soon as it stopped they would sit down and rest. This was the most animated and interesting of all the dances. The Indians, daubed with the rusty-red clay, bearing their grotesque and hideous masks, and armed with long spears from which flaunted coloured streamers, rushed hither and thither, charging the spectator as if an infuriated buffalo were about to impale him upon his horns, and, with the cessation of the drumming, sank, exhausted to the ground. The airs the musicians sang for this dance were really very tuneful, and were an inspiration to the dancers.

Another dance was called the Lodge Dance, so named because it was always carried on in a large lodge made of many wigwam coverings and their poles. This was for the young men and women of the tribes, the only old Indians taking part in it being the musicians and drummers.

There were other dances of no real importance, which any Indian could begin--for instance, the "Giving-away Dance," which would be started by some Indian who happened to have something he wished to give to some friend of his. He would take a small flat drum, and with his hand beat an accompaniment to a song, the words of which would mean that the present he was giving was the very best of its kind to be had, was new and was very useful. The recipient would have to give something in exchange, and in a little while almost every Indian in the camp would be seen bobbing up and down to the time of the beating of the drum and the song of the "Giving-away Dance."

The Indians have a keen sense of humour, and many of them would make up the most ridiculous words in praise of some article they were giving away, and thus cause no end of amusement to the onlookers. To such an extreme was this dance carried at times, that some of the Indians would give away almost everything they possessed, so that it was a positive blessing when rain came and put a stop to it.

Then there was another dance called the Round Dance, which was for the women of the tribe only. They danced in a small circle to their own singing and drumming. This was a very pretty dance, as the women and girls were always dressed in their very best, with faces painted and hair smoothly brushed and plaited; they were very picturesque and graceful in their movements.

Then there was the "Cannibal Dance," taken part in altogether by the old men. They would try to make themselves as hideous as possible (and that was not much of an effort) and would hop and limp around to their own "singing," which consisted of groans and other peculiar noises. They took great pleasure in this dance, and caused much merriment to the rest of the band.

Chapter 4

THE INDIANS WHO WERE KNOWN AS "MEDICINE MEN" were looked upon as possessing all sorts of peculiar gifts and powers. First of all came their knowledge of the curative properties of many different roots and herbs. In many cases these medicine men did understand their medicinal qualities, but others again worked upon the faith of their patients to a great extent. It is to be feared many Indians were not entitled to the amount of honour they received by virtue of their title of Muskick-kee-wee-ni-nee" (Medicine Man).

The real medicine man began early in life to make a study of curing the sick by the use of roots and herbs, and seldom made use of the unnecessary amount of noise from drums and rattles (see-see-quans) which so many of them used in trying to cure their patients. In the prescriptions of roots and herbs the old women of the band were very often more to be trusted than the men. The cures these old women effected were in many cases wonderful.

It often happened that an Indian and his wife worked together in the healing of the sick, and it was usually expected that the best results would be achieved by these companions in the healing art. These two Indians would keep very much to themselves, and could be seen at any hour of the day, from sunrise to sunset, digging and searching for their roots and herbs. After finding them they would dry them, either in the sun or by the camp fire, and, after they were dry, they would tie them up in little round parcels. The wrappings were usually made of soft deerskin, tied with strings of the same material. The outside of each bundle was always coloured in different hues, and they could, therefore, be easily distinguished one from another. For example, all the medicine for headache was parcelled up in little red bundles, that for colds in yellow bundles; the colour on the outside of each was as good as a label. All these parcels were kept in a large medicine bag, also made of leather and decorated with all manner of crude drawings, but principally by the outline of the medicine man's "Pow-wah-kun," or dream. This medicine bag was kept hanging on a pole outside the medicine man's wigwam; no other sign was necessary to show you where the gifted Indian lived or camped.

When he was not engaged looking for medicinal herbs the medicine man was shut up in his wigwam singing different weird songs and incantations to his particular

Pow-wah-kun to bring him greater skill in his profession or calling. They were not supposed to be interrupted during these secret ceremonies.

The more reserved of the medicine men and women were respected according to their exclusiveness, and were only approached in time of great necessity. These old Indians always made use of the medicine rattles (see-see-quans) and, if called upon to cure any really sick person they would sing and rattle these little see-see-quans right over the head of the patient. These remedial rites were practised in case of fever and delirium especially. Such a noise did they make in the wigwam of the poor unfortunate Indian that it is a wonder he ever survived a "treatment" by these old medicine men.

In explaining their reasons for using the see-see-quans and drums over a sick person, an old Indian said: "When it has been very hot during the summer for days at a time, all the flowers, trees, and grasses droop and fade. Now to revive these the Great Spirit sends the thunder and lightning and rain, and in a little while all nature is refreshed and lives again. He awakens them with the thunder, we try to awaken our sick with the see-see-quans and drums, and at the same time give him medicine to drink, just as the Great Spirit sends the rain to help the drooping leaves and grass."

When a person became delirious or demented the Indians imagined him possessed of the spirit of a cannibal (Ween-de-go), and if the unfortunate patient remained delirious for any length of time he was usually killed by being burned. The medicine man confessed himself baffled by delirium, or any alienation of the mind, and after trying without success to give some relief to the afflicted person, would warn his friends that unless some Indian or member of his family, who was known to be on unfriendly terms with the patient, did not come forward and help do away with the Ween-de-go, the bad spirit would enter into him. The Indians had strong superstitions regarding cannibals and lunatics, and with tears in their eyes would help burn the poor patient. The Indians, having no asylums or any means of isolating their unfortunate lunatics, were compelled to do away with them. It was utterly impossible for an Indian to go on a hunting expedition and leave his family to the mercy of a lunatic; so that any person showing marked signs of insanity was dispatched by his sorrowing and superstitious friends. Fortunately, years ago there was very little fever, and, consequently, less delirium amongst the Indians.

The medicine man was often appealed to by Indians who were unfortunate in their love affairs. He was supposed to have medicine or charms which would bring about the desired results. If any young woman knew her rejected suitor had gone to the medicine man (and the information was usually conveyed to her), she at once tried to treat her lover more kindly. And this was supposed to be the result of the "medicine," whereas it was really the fear of harm from the old medicine man which brought about the change. The medicine used on these occasions was sprinkled liberally over two little wooden images, supposed to represent the young man and woman whose love was not reciprocal. After they had been sprinkled with the medicine, some hair from the head of the person whose love was desired would be bound around the two images, and then they would be wrapped up in fine deerskin. They would be carried about by the person who was desirous of being loved. Then the information was conveyed that the medicine man had made "love medicine," and, as has been said before, the results were usually satisfactory. If they were not, the two little images would be thrown away, and, in consequence, the person for whom the "love medicine" was intended would suffer for years with very severe headaches. This is the reason why Indians were always so careful to burn any hair which they lost from their heads (the scalp lock excepted; it could not be destroyed, and it was seldom combed after once being plaited and tied into position).

Another peculiar medicine which was very much dreaded by the Indians was a "bad medicine" (Muchie-mus-kee-kee) which made them turn black and caused a growth of down to appear all over their faces. This was the revenge taken by some Indian who had suffered any real or imaginary wrong at the hands of another. The poor Indian who was afflicted by this form of poison was disfigured for life, and if he or she had ever possessed any attractiveness it was most effectively obliterated. A strange thing in connection with this phase of poisoning was that the medicine men and women were more often poisoned than any other members of the tribe. This may be accounted for by the unusual amount of jealousy which existed among them. As a matter of fact, there was more unfriendliness between the medicine men than among all the rest of the tribe. The Indians, as a rule, were most friendly and kind to each other, but were very sensitive, and often took exception to remarks made by thoughtless persons who had really intended no harm, but caused it by their tactlessness. If the remarks caused him to be ridiculed the injured person would frequently brood over the gossip or jibe until it assumed such importance that he would strive to be revenged, and would consult the medicine man, who would administer the poison. It was no wonder, then, that the respect which the medicine men should have commanded was so often tinged with fear.

Though they charged as much as they could possibly get from their patients, the medicine men never dressed as well as as the other Indians. It was a common thing to hear of an Indian paying the medicine man for his services with a pony, or even two. Yet when the band was travelling from one point to another the medicine man would usually tramp along laden with his impedimenta while the rest of the band rode on ponies.

A noticeable possession of the medicine man was his collection of canines. One might well wonder where an Indian could possibly have gathered so many specimens of that animal, and why he kept them. The dogs were so ugly and vicious that they served their master as a body-guard; no one could approach him or his wigwam without raising a loud protest from them. So when any Indian wished to visit the medicine man he had to summon his courage and arm himself with a good stout stick. The most aggravating part of the visit would be the utter indifference of the old medicine man to the yelping and snarling of his dogs and to the discomfort of his visitor. Not until the very last minute would the dogs be remonstrated with by their owner. The old medicine women would have even a larger number of these dogs, and if possible, a more vicious lot. One can readily understand, then, how easy it was for these old Indians to keep to themselves. The wigwam of the medicine man was really the only one in the whole encampment which was not entered without "knocking at the door," so to speak.

In the years long past, when our Indians were at war with so many other tribes, it was customary to keep a great many dogs around each camping-ground, so that they would sound an alarm at the approach of the enemy. But latterly these were kept by the medicine men and women only, for though there are usually any number of dogs roaming around an encampment of Indians, the most of them will invariably be found to belong to that particular class of old Indian. In fact, it is impossible to imagine these Indians without their faithful, if noisy, companions.

As has been said before, the medicine man was usually feared quite as much, if not more, than respected; and there were many Indians who tried in different ways to make existence for them unpleasant, especially for those who were known to be too free with their knowledge of "bad medicine." They would often find themselves minus a pony which perhaps only a few days before had been received in payment for administering poison to some unfortunate.

There were, nevertheless, many of the old medicine men and women who were loved and respected by the band, and who never made use of their knowledge to hurt or injure others by harmful medicines. These old Indians did all they possibly could to alleviate the ills and afflictions of their patients, and some of the cures they wrought were really wonderful.

A great many of their methods of treating the sick will remain unknown to us, as they are, with many other practices, a thing of the past. It is very doubtful if the medicine man ever revealed to any white man all the secrets of his healing art. It was such a solemn thing to them that they very seldom spoke of it even among themselves; so very naturally they would be even more reticent about it when with strangers. There is no doubt that many of their methods, such as bleeding and the vapour baths, were copied by any of the Indians who felt they could safely employ these means of lessening their ills, but there were many things known only to the medicine man which will never be known to anyone else. That some of these old Indians devoted their lives to the healing of their sick goes without saying, and that they looked to the Great Spirit for His blessing and assistance is also very true of those Indians who did so much to alleviate the ills of their race. They tried to do good, and in many cases accomplished much, for which they earned the gratitude of the members of their band. They firmly believed that Kichie Manitou had planted in the ground all manner of healing things, and if they only could find them and use them there would never be any sickness among the Indians. Many of them devoted their lives to searching for those healing plants; and when they were nearing the end of their journey on this earth would remind those who were following in their calling to keep up the good work, as they felt there was so much more to be discovered than they had found.

Surely the journey of these old Indians to the Happy Hunting Gounds was made pleasant for them by the Great Spirit who watched over all their patients, and gave them knowledge to do good when they appealed to Him.

Years ago there was comparatively little sickness among the Indians. The outdoor life they led, the food they ate, everything made for a healthful existence. One never heard of epidemics breaking out among the Indians then. They kept themselves clean, and never stayed for any length of time in one camping-place. They moved their tepees on an average two or three times a week in the summer season, and in winter would have a plentiful supply of clean spruce boughs or hay and moss, with which they would cover the ground in their tepees; and this was changed every few days to ensure cleanliness. If it were known that an Indian did not keep his tepee in a clean and fresh condition he was avoided by the rest of the band, and, if necessary, was told why. In this way, it was easy to keep up their standard of health.

Long ago the Indians used to indulge in a vapour bath which they called ma-too-tah-win. This bath was taken in a small tent covered securely with buffalo robes. The steam or vapour was obtained by pouring water on a few large stones which had previously been heated and placed in a hole in the ground inside the little tent. Even now one may see occasionally a place where an Indian had enjoyed his Turkish bath. The "ma-too-tah-wee-ca-mick," or vapour lodge, was built by bending strong and supple boughs of the willow, and sticking the larger ends firmly into the ground, forming a circle, the smaller ends being tied or braided at the top. This was four or even six feet in diameter and about three feet high. It was covered by buffalo robes or dressed leather, having a small opening by which the Indian crawled inside; this he did after the hot stones had been rolled into the hole made for them. After he was inside the little lodge, a vessel containing some water would be handed him, and the opening or door securely closed. Then, when undressed, he would splash the water on the hot stones, causing the steam to rise. The Indian would remain in the tent for quite a long time afterwards, in order to avoid taking cold. They claimed this vapour bath rid their bodies of any impurities and fortified them against diseases.

Their food was always nourishing; the main part of it consisted of buffalo meat. dried and pounded, or powdered and made into pemmican. They also used a great quantity of dried fruits, and occasionally wild rice (*Zizania aquatica*)—an ideal food, being sufficiently rich and starchy to constitute a perfect diet in itself.

Chapter 5

• The buffalo • Hunting on the plains • Method of dressing the hides • Embroidery
and dyeing • Picture writing • Pemmican and other food preparations.

WHAT THE INDIANS DID NOT OWE TO THE BUFFALO one can hardly imagine. This noble beast provided them with almost everything they required in the olden times. Every part of its flesh was converted into food, dried and preserved so that it could be kept for months and even years, without losing any of its nutritive qualities, and on it they could subsist entirely, if they were not in a position to obtain any of the wild vegetation which constituted the cereal part of their food. The hides of the animals were worn instead of blankets, which they never saw until the white man brought them into their country. The buffalo skins were also tanned or dressed into soft leather, which they used in making their wigwams or tepees, and for their bedding. The buffalo skins when dressed and smoked were used for their clothing and footwear. The untanned skins or parchments, were used to make their saddles and bridles, and for lassoes and thongs. The horns were shaped into spoons and drinking cups. The brains were used in the tanning of the skins. The bones were used for the different implements required in the tanning and dressing of the skins, for saddle horns, and for war clubs. The bones were also crushed, and all the marrow fat contained in them was boiled or melted out. The sinews were dried and used for makng thread for sewing their garments, as well as for strings for their bows. The feet and hoofs were boiled for the glue they contained, which the Indians used for fastening their arrow points and for other purposes. The long hair from the head and shoulders was twisted and plaited into halters, and the tail was used for a brush with which to kill flies and mosquitoes.

The Indians took great pride in the skill required to kill these animals, and were justly proud when they possessed a strong, swift pony, trained to run after the buffalo. As the latter often showed fight when hard pressed, the ponies required to be very well trained indeed, and the Indian to have more than ordinary courage. It was no mean accomplishment to be a good buffalo hunter; and one can imagine no greater sport than that of a genuine buffalo hunt, as indulged in years ago by the Indians. In those days the noble animal of the plains travelled over the prairies in great herds, and often the Indians would have to ride for miles after them in order to get near enough to be able to kill them with their bows and arrows, or spears. When guns and rifles were first introduced it revolutionized the buffalo hunt, and helped to exterminate these animals, as the Indians soon became very skilled in the use of these weapons. The bow and arrow, however, was the favourite weapon for hunting the buffalo, as it was swift and silent. The Indians have been known to shoot an arrow through one animal and into another. One cannot write of the Indians of the prairies without mentioning the buffalo; and anyone interested in the former must regret the extermination of the latter. One can sympathize with the older Indians, types of a dying race, in their lament for the days gone by when they were the sole inhabitants of the vast prairies in the West, free to roam wherever they felt inclined to go; free to hunt the buffalo and other game, which they firmly believed were there only for their use, provided by the Great Spirit, who took such care of them.

One old Indian, in speaking of their early life as he knew it, said: "They were wealthy because they had all they could possibly desire. They were happy because they were healthy, and had such a beautiful country. Kichie Manitou took care of them in those days. He held them in the palm of His hand, as if they were frail as an eggshell; when there were storms and tempests, and in the winter time, He would cover them with His other hand and shield them from all harm." To a people who believed so firmly in the goodness and protection of the Great Spirit that they turned to Him for every little want, whose faith in Him was beyond the ordinary conception of the word, came the white man, and, alas, with his coming came their undoing.

Certainly it would appear that the white men helped to exterminate the buffalo, which provided the Indians with food and raiment, by buying as many of the robes as they could possibly get, out of season as well as in season. The Indians would kill hundreds of them just for their pelts alone.

The hides were dressed in the following manner by the Indian women. After the hide had been taken from the animal, it was hung over the branch of a tree and a sharp instrument was used to scrape off any fat or flesh adhering to the skin. This little implement, usually made from the lower bone of the foreleg of the animal, had nicked or serrated edges at the wider end of the bone, which had first been filed down as flat and as sharp as possible. The part used as a handle was bound around by a throng of dressed buffalo skin, with a loop at the end into which the arm was slipped, to enable it to be more securely held by the operator. After all the fat and flesh had been removed from the skin, it was stretched flat on the ground, with the skin next to the earth, and left there till dried by the heat of the sun. When it was perfectly dry, and the hide was to be dressed or tanned into leather, the hair was scraped off by another sharp instrument, resembling a small hoe, and made from the horn of an elk, the crook in the horn being filed down flat and as sharp as it could be made. The filing was done by stones, the only thing they could use for this purpose years ago. This little tool was used by the Indian women with a peculiar swaying motion of the holy, and it was surprising how quickly every particle of the hair was removed from the skin. In this state it was called parchment, and was used to make thongs and lassoes, and also to make canoes or boats.

After all the hair was removed, the parchment was hung or placed on poles over a fire for a few minutes, and then taken down, spread on the ground again, and grease sprinkled over it, usually squirted through the mouth of the person tanning it. Then it was again placed on the poles over the fire, and left until the grease was perfectly absorbed. Great care was taken all the time it was hanging over the fire not to scorch the parchment in the least, as that, of course, would ruin it.

After the grease had been thoroughly absorbed by the skin or hide a mixture composed of the brains of the buffalo and wormwood (*Artemisia absinthium*) was rubbed well into the hide, and left for a short time to be absorbed by it, and when this was partially accomplished the cooked liver of the animal, after it had been crushed and pounded up, usually by a flat stone in a shallow vessel made of clay or birch bark, was rubbed or spread all over it, and a few minutes after warm water was gently poured on the shin until it was thoroughly soaked through. It was then folded up and left over night. The next morning it would be hung over a pole or strong line, and all the brain, wormwood and liver would be carefully scraped off. It was then washed and wrung out perfectly dry. This wringing was done by passing the folded hide around a strong post or small tree and around a short, stout stick of about a yard in length, which would be twisted in the hands of the tanner until almost every particle of moisture was squeezed or wrung out of it. After this it was hung out in the sun and allowed to dry, but during this process of drying it was frequently taken down and rubbed through a hoop made of coarse sinew, so that when it was dry the skin was almost as soft as flannel. This final process was really the most tedious part of the whole work, as it would take hours to thoroughly soften it. The older the animal, the more tedious would be the softening process.

The leather was always comparatively white, but if it was to be used for making moccasins or other wearing apparel it was smoked. The smoking was done by stitching up the skin on the form of a bag, building a fire, or rather, smudge, of decayed or rotten wood, and stretching the bag over it; the bag being held firmly in place by small poles, and pegged securely to the ground over the smudge, which was built in a small round hole in the ground. None of the smoke was allowed to escape. After one side had been thoroughly smoked and had taken on a rich golden brown colour, the bag would be removed, turned inside out, placed over the smudge again, and that side also thoroughly smoked. This finish by smoking would ensure the leather being kept perfectly soft after any number of contacts with rain and water.

When the Indians made their wigwams or tepees of the leather, it was used without being smoked, as the fires which were built in their tepees very soon did all that was necessary in that particular. The hides of the wapiti, moose and deer made a much softer leather after being dressed and smoked than that of the buffalo, but were not so durable. In dressing the buffalo pelts for robes they went through the same process of tanning, but the hair was not removed.

In cases where the leather was required for ornamented apparel and trimmings it was dyed with different roots and clays. When this coloured leather was embroidered with quills from the porcupine, and beaded, and decorated with shells, it could be employed in making picturesque and effective garments. As the Indians were all very fond of gay colours, and used them in artistic combinations, they presented when dressed in their best a barbaric and brilliant spectacle.

They also made use of the dyes which they obtained from the roots of different shrubs and plants, in ornamenting their tepees or wigwams and in painting upon them the notable events in the careers of their owners.

Every Indian of note drew and coloured the form of his guardian spirit or Pow-wah-kun on different parts of his tepee or wigwam. In some cases this form or figure would occupy almost a quarter of the space, and around it would be grouped crude drawings illustrating the history of the Indian, principally events in his career as a warrior. These adventures were supposed to have called for great daring and courage, and the illustrations or drawings were a silent but effective way of showing. what manner of man the Indian was. It was an easy matter for a tactful visitor to make a remark which would lead the conversation to his host's many deeds of bravery. Once that topic was introduced one could spend hours listening to some interesting reminiscences. And the introduction of the subject was taken as a mark of courtesy and appreciation on the part of the visitor.

The Indians preserved every bit of the flesh of the buffalo, and though this was a very simple process it was nevertheless a wonderfully effective one. If during the very hottest part of the summer the Indians killed ten, twenty or even many more buffalo, not a pound of flesh was allowed to spoil. The bones were also crushed, and all the marrow fat extracted from them. This was done by boiling the bones in sufficient water to cover them, and as the marrow or grease rose to the surface it was carefully skimmed off and poured into the bladder of the buffalo after it had been thoroughly washed and cleaned. This fat was eaten with "pounded meat," and was also used in the making of pemmican.

The flesh of the buffalo was cut off the bones and sliced into very thin layers by the Indian women, every woman in the band taking part in this work when necessary. After being cut as thin as possible into sheets (often measuring twenty-four by thirty-six inches), the meat was dried by being hung on a scaffolding of poles erected over a fire which was kept burning until the drying and smoking process was accomplished. This fire together with the intense rays of the sun quickly dried the meat, which was turned frequently to allow of an even distribution of heat and smoke, both being necessary for its complete preservation. This was the way they made "dried meat," and in this form it could be kept for years, retaining all its nourishment.

When this was to be converted into "pounded meat" for pemmican, etc., it was placed on parchment hides, and with a flail pounded into a fine powder. For pemmican the Indians would mix into this "pounded meat" sufficient marrow fat to form the whole into the consistency required for packing. This resembled flour "shortened" for "puff paste"; the colour of it was a yellowish brown. In this form it was packed very tightly into strong parchment bags of a uniform size, which were sewn up with thread made of sinew, which was also obtained from the buffalo.

An inferior grade of pemmican was made by using coarser "pounded meat," together with "drippings" made of the rendered fat of the animal.

The Indians also made a very fine pemmican with the "pounded meat," marrow fat, and dried fruits, such as the saskatoomin (a blueberry) and crushed chokecherries.

The favorite part of the buffalo flesh was that cut off the "boss" or "hump." The meat was cut into small pieces, then smoked and dried in the usual way. In this form it was called "chee-sa-wa-nah," and was delicious.

The tongue of the buffalo was dried in the same way, and could be kept for years in any climate without losing its flavor.

The buffalo sinew which the Indians used for sewing their garments and wigwams, for making strings for their bows, etc., was taken from the shoulder blade, and back part of the animal. It was very carefully cut out, all the flesh scraped off, then it was dried, after which it was ready for use.

Chapter 6

THE COURAGE AND DARING OF THE INDIANS HAS OFTEN been discussed, and usually very much to their disadvantage; but anyone knowing them well would never question their bravery.

The Indians of our Western Provinces always wore in a plait a small portion of their hair, gathered from a spot at the crown of the head, about the size of a silver dollar. Many may have noticed this peculiar style of hair-dressing, yet may never have understood its significance. To wear it was a sign of bravery, for there it fluttered in the sight of the foe, inciting him to closest combat for the possession of this proud crest. Naturally an Indian considered it a grave misfortune to lose his scalp, but it was a greater disgrace not to have the scalp-lock ready from the day he was able to take part in any fighting. The scalp-lock was also very much ornamented. After being separated from the rest of the hair, the lock was plaited and twined around with strips of fur, preferably otter, ermine, mink or beaver, and then decorated with beads or porcupine quills. Very often a shell or small brass disc would be slipped over the plait and fastened securely against the head. In war time the scalp-lock was very conspicuous by its decoration, and was worn in that fashion as a special incitement to the foe. During the dangers and excitement of forays or battles they never showed an atom of fear. They made ideal scouts; and that alone called for great bravery and courage. One has often heard of small expeditions led by certain Indians accomplishing wonderful feats of bravery, and defeating overwhelmingly larger numbers of the enemy, returning with scores of horses in triumph to their friends. These raids were often the result of trivial bets between certain members of the band, but, in the event, they furnished evidence of the stuff the Indian was made of.

That they had no fear of death, but indeed, often seemed to court it, may in a measure be accounted for by their ideas of the life beyond; this earthly life being considered only as of short duration, and at best full of trials and sorrows, while the life in the Happy Hunting Grounds was supposed to be perfect, with no enemies to fight, no parting from loved ones, game in abundance, and never any fear of famine.

The courage displayed at the time of the Sun Dance, when they endured cruel self-inflicted tortures, is another indication of bravery. Where else could one find so many candidates for such a test of courage and endurance as among these Indians?

Before closing this subject mention must be made of their wonderfully heroic

Cree Indian with travois.

endurance of pain. One can easily imagine what this must have been when years ago they suffered so often from broken limbs. This was only too common an occurrence in the days when they hunted the buffalo over the prairies. Mounted upon their fleet-footed ponies, racing after their game, it very often happened that both rider and pony would be laid low by the latter stepping into a badger's hold, or other sudden depression in the ground. Though the Indians were splendid riders, and their ponies wonderfully clever in avoiding these holes, the excitement of the chase made it almost impossible for the horse to keep clear of all such pitfalls, and the rider, intent on taking aim at a buffalo, would perhaps be forgetful of the dangers of riding on the prairies, and thus the two would often be thrown to the hard ground with disastrous results to both. In the days when the killing was done with bow and arrow and spear, it was bad enough when the rider was not hurled among the buffalo; if an Indian was thrown he usually fell among the herd, and was rescued with difficulty by his companions, and often not before he had sustained serious injuries. These wounds, abrasions, or fractures were bandaged up by some of the Indians, very seldom by the medicine men, who were not, as a rule, very proficient in surgery. The poor Indians would suffer greatly from these broken limbs and the rough treatment which was intended to repair them, more especially during the heat of summer, but they endured all the pain and discomfort with great fortitude; in fact, with never a murmur or sound of complaint. And in all other cases of suffering they showed the same silent and uncomplaining patience.

They also displayed great endurance when running after game on foot. Many Indians in the old days did not possess a horse or pony of any description, so would have to depend upon their own fleetness of foot to catch up with the buffalo or deer.

This meant running for hours at a time, no mean feat, over prairie covered by a heavy growth of grass, which grew to enormous height on the plains, but which also helped to conceal the Indian so that he was often enabled to approach to within shooting distance of his game. This was often done at a time when the killing of a few buffalo or deer meant the saving of their families from starvation, perhaps after days of necessary fasting, which would, of course, test their strength as well as powers of endurance.

There is at the present time an Indian, Acoose, at the Crooked Lakes Agency in Saskatchewan, on Sakimay's (Mosquito) Reserve, who in the year 1884 ran after seven jumping deer from Moose Mountain to a point where the present agency buildings at Crooked Lakes stand. He had exhausted his ammunition at Moose Mountain, and the only place where he could obtain a further supply was at the Hudson's Bay Company's post on the reserve. Here he got more powder and ball for an old-fashioned but highly prized muzzle-loading gun, and killed all the deer, after a run of nearly a hundred miles. This Indian comes of a well known family of runners and hunters; his father being one of the very oldest Indians alive, at this time (1907) aged 102. Qui-witch is a name well known to the past two generations, as its possessor was one of the bravest Indians, and has seen many wonderful changes on the western prairies. He is a remarkably intelligent old man, and though he has suffered complete loss of eyesight, is most interested in all things concerning the welfare of his fellow Indians. His sons were brave men in the days of their warfare with the Blackfoot and other nations, and were handsome specimens of the Saulteaux.

Many such personal examples might be cited in support of the courage and endurance of the Indians. Piapot's name should be mentioned as a brave warrior; he was of Cree and Assiniboine extraction. Muscowpetung (Saulteaux) is another old Indian whose name was always spoken when brave men were named. Kak-keeg-ca-way (Voice of an Eagle) is another valiant Saulteaux. These Indians and many others are still alive, whose deeds of bravery, courage and endurance would inspire even a coward to do things he never would have dreamed of doing without their example. In another chapter will be found some particular anecdotes of the courageous dead, the great Koo-min-ah-koush, the intrepid Yellow-Head, and the cunning Chim-ass-cous.

The women of these tribes were also very brave, and did much to help their husbands, brothers and friends to victory when hard pressed by the enemy. Many women, indeed, took part in these fights when the men were outnumbered, and by their daring and courage often turned the tide in their favour. But the women never spoke of any such exploits, and were ever most modest as to their acts of bravery and courage in rendering assistance when necessity compelled them to do so.

To see the many privations and hardships of the Indian women and children even at the present day is to realize how much they must formerly have suffered in times of sickness. But they endured everything most uncomplainingly, and often had to travel with the band when they should have been resting. Usually, if there was any sickness in the camp travelling was only done under compulsion. If they were being hard pressed by their enemies they would have to keep moving in the hope of falling in with friendly tribes. Upon these occasions the sick and wounded would have to be moved too, and with their crude modes of transportation these forced marches were most painful and trying ordeals for the sufferers, whose endurance was truly heroic.

Chapter 7

NOT THE LEAST INTERESTING FEATURE OF THE LIFE of the Indian was his mode of travelling. They took the greatest possible comfort out of the camper's life, and had all its procedure reduced to a science. They could "pitch camp" in a few minutes and be on their way to some other place in a wonderfully short space of time. In camping and travelling they had a place for everything and everything was always in its place, and this, more than anything else, made for comfort and dispatch. They had the happy knack of making the best use of everything, and this quality helped them in no small degree when inconveniences were unexpectedly met with. Anyone who had "camped out" and travelled to any extent in the West before railways and stages had appeared would recall this resourcefulness and quick adaptability.

Years ago the Indians did not have in their equipment the historic "Red River cart," which in after years was to them such a necessary conveyance. In its place they used the "travois," a conveyance formed of two poles, very light and strong, tied together a foot or two from the smaller ends with buffalo thongs, in such a way as to form a saddle which rested upon the horse's back. Two cross-pieces, about three feet apart, towards the larger ends of the poles, gave firmness to the contrivance, and between these lower pieces would be slung a shallow basket made of thongs or rawhide, which could bear a weight of two hundred pounds or more.

Upon this they would pack their wigwams and other possessions, the basket being far enough from the larger ends of the poles to prevent its touching the ground when loaded to its full capacity. A much smaller "travois" was made for their dogs to haul, these useful little animals being as a rule the only ones used by the older women of the tribes, as they were more easily managed than the ponies. The dogs were the primitive travois-bearers, and even after the introduction of ponies were often used by a whole band to convey their goods and chattels after a successful raid by an enemy, who might perhaps have captured every pony they possessed.

Although the invention of the travois is obvious when the conditions under which it was evolved are considered, yet it was nicely adapted for its various functions, which are thus described by Mr. Geo. B. Grinnell:

> On the platform of the travois are carried loads of meat from the buffalo-killing, the
> various possessions of the owner in moving camp from place to place, a sick or

wounded individual too weak to ride, and sometimes a wickerwork cage shaped like a sweat lodge, in which are confined small children, or even a family of tiny puppies with their mother. Things that cannot be conveniently packed on the backs of the horses are put upon the travois. Sometimes the travois bears the dead, for with certain tribes it is essential to the future welfare of the departed that they be brought back to the tribal burying-ground near the village.*

When the Indian travelled at leisure he always chose some particularly pictur-esque place in which to camp; and the young men, who generally rode ahead of the band, were always on the watch for a suitable camping-ground. If, with its other attractions, it had good water, the band would stay there for weeks at a time, send-ing out hunting and raiding expeditions. Here they would stay and put up provisions for the winter; the men hunted the buffalo while the women made dried meat, pem-mican and marrow fat, and dressed or tanned the hides into leather and robes. If the hunt was successful, the women world make new tepees or wigwams, and this was very interesting, as many willing workers would offer their help in sewing up the skins required for the tents. It was customary to have a feast upon the completion of the work, and all the women of the band were bidden to this ceremony; no men ever attended. In making the wigwam, a level piece of ground would be found, and on this would be spread the skins; as many as twenty were required for a large tent, but ten, twelve and fourteen skins went to make the ordinary size. While the skins were being picked over and spread out on the ground, the expert woman who did the cutting-out was busily engaged sharpening her knife, in fact four or five knives would be sharpened in readiness for use, as one after the other became dulled by cut-ting the thick leather. While all this was going on a group of the women would be making the sinews for the sewing, so that once the actual work began, it took only a few hours for the wigwam to be finished. The sewing was done on each seam or piece as it lay on the ground, necessitating the sewer doing her work in a stooping position. None of the threads of sinew were cut off, even if a piece ten inches long was left over. If the ends of the sinews were cut off the occupants of the wigwam were supposed to become very stingy and mean in all their dealings, and indeed might actually want for the common necessities of life before the tent was worn out.

After all the sewing and trimming, such as fringes, etc., were finished, the women were asked to partake of refreshments in the form of fine dried meat, pemmican, chee-sa-wa-nah, and smoked tongue and tea. This latter beverage was obtained years ago from the swamp-shrub known as Labrador Tea (*Ledum latifolium*). This the Indians called Medicine water (Mus-kic-kee-wa-poo) and it certainly tasted like medicine. They liked the flavour of it very much, however, and as it was not easily obtained, appreciated it when they got it. The old women of the band generally col-lected this plant from swamps in parts of the country where there were pine forests, and after gathering it, would dry it carefully, and pack it in air-tight parchment bags. These bags were in fact the complete skin of an unborn calf obtained from a buffa-lo cow that had been killed. The skin was taken from the animal with only one inci-sion, through which every part of the body was drawn. This small hide was washed and during the drying was rubbed soft, without undergoing any of the usual process of tanning or dressing given the larger skins. Being completely air-tight, it answered

---

* George B. Grinnell, *The Story of the Indian* (New York: Appleton's, 1895).

admirably the purpose for which it was used. Many an old woman took pride in having two or three of these skins packed so full of this tea that they resembled the original shape of the little animal. There are a few of these bags still to be seen, which their owners prize very highly.

The decorating or painting of the tepees was always done by the braves, who took great pride in the crude drawings on the white leather, illustrating the principal deeds of bravery and prowess to the credit of their owners. Sometimes the illustrations would refer to an especially successful hunting expedition, perhaps after days of fasting by the band, which made it an event of no small importance in the Indian's career. The principal drawing, however, was always of the dream (Pow-wah-kun) or guardian spirit; this always occupied a most prominent place among the drawings and was also traced over the door of the tent.

These tepees or wigwams were most comfortable and roomy, and could be kept fresh and clean; the opening at the top of the doorway caused a constant current of air, and they were very healthy places of abode. In rainy weather and also in the autumn and winter, fires were kept burning in the very centre, the smoke escaping through the opening at the top by means of the ears or wings of the tent, a sort of rude chimney-jack which the occupants very easily arranged, with poles that were stuck into the small pockets of the ears. These ears acted as a shield against the breezes and permitted the smoke to escape. In warm weather, the caves of the tent were always drawn up a foot or two from the ground, causing a constant circulation of pure air. No Indian ever kept his wigwam standing on one place for more than a few days at a time, as the grass was soon trampled into the earth, giving an untidy appearance to the interior of the tent; so, to avoid this, they kept constantly changing the teepee from one place to another, within a certain radius.

Having secured a pleasant camping-ground, the Indians would spend their time in many useful ways. When the men were not off on a hunting expedition they would be busy mending harness, or making new sets; repairing their saddles, which were made of buffalo leather; or years ago, before they had rifles and guns, in making bows and arrows. These required the greatest amount of labour, as in their strength lay all safety and sustenance. The bows were made from the cherry tree, which is strong and supple, and the arrows from the saskatoomin tree.

While the men were thus engaged, the women were busily employed in the making of dried meat, pemmican and marrow fat, in tanning and dressing the leather, making moccasins, and other sewing. They also carried all the water and wood they used. One must bear in mind, however, that the carrying of wood was no great hardship, as they used very little fuel during the summer, especially on the prairies, where they had only scrub and willow to burn, often indeed not even these; then they had to use the dry buffalo "chips" (excrement). And during the winter weather, if the women had to haul, or carry on their backs, any wood, it was always of the very lightest kind, and they never overburdened themselves. The heavy logs required during the cold weather were drawn to the camp by horses; and the younger men did all the chopping and cutting. Of course, there were times when this work had to be done by the women, when the men were away on their hunting trips, but only when the supply provided by the men was exhausted. The popular idea of the poor Indian woman doing all the hard work has too often been overdrawn.

In the evening, when their day's work was done, they exchanged visits, and over the camp fires many interesting reminiscences were recalled and discussed by the men, the women being at such times very attentive listeners. One sometimes met with a particularly interesting old woman whose life had been passed in keen observation of all the triumphs and trials of her band, who in a quiet and gentle manner would recount the many events she had lived through. These were at times most thrilling, relating to narrow escapes from the merciless clutches of their enemies, the Blackfoot and other nations, who were most cruel and powerful adversaries, and who from all accounts made life most precarious for the Crees, Saulteaux and Assiniboines. During the summer no stories founded on fiction were ever told; the Indians, with their intensely superstitious natures, believing that if any "fairy" tales were told during that season when they were supposed to use all their time to the very best advantage, the narrator would have his or her life destroyed by the lizard, which would suck all his blood. The Indians very naturally were in terror of this little reptile, which was never actually known to have been the cause of any loss of life among them; but they assert as a reason for this that no Indian ever gave it an opportunity to put to the test its evil powers. So in the long summer evenings, only actual happenings in their lives were recited. The younger women of the band would at that time of the day do fancy-work, which they looked upon as a recreation. And in those days every brave had at least one costume, covered with porcupine quill-work, and with gaily coloured seed beads when these were obtainable.

The Indian women displayed much artistic taste in their fancy-work. Their designs were perfect as to detail. The bead and quill work done upon finely dressed deerskin, or even soft buffalo skin, was almost everlasting, the stitching and threading of the beads and quills being done with fine sinew. The garments were unfortunately subjected to the very hardest wear, in all kinds of weather, during the four seasons. But even under these conditions they lasted for a very long time. The moccasins were always finished with a partially softened parchment sole, which added months to their wearing qualities.

Such an encampment amid beautiful scenery, astir with prosperous and contented Indians, must have been a most striking illustration of the Indians' own idea of the wonderful love and care bestowed upon them by the Great Spirit. It is no wonder that they believed so fully in His care and keeping.

There are quite a number of Indians still living in our Western Provinces who remember the time when they enjoyed just such an existence, and whose recollections are most interesting.

The young children played their games amidst these lovely scenes; the little babes, tied up in the mossbag or Indian cradle, awoke from their slumbers and looked upon the joyous and happy lives of their brothers and sisters, and grew up to appreciate everything which made life so pleasant an existence for their tribe. From the first they were taught how much they owed to the Great Spirit for all His blessings. They wanted for nothing. If there were times when the game was scarce and food insufficient they willingly endured privations, never murmuring; satisfied to hunt patiently until the Great Spirit again sent the buffalo and deer to appease their hunger.

They had many trials and difficulties in their travels, but these they made light of, and did their best to make themselves comfortable, no matter what might betide.

Perhaps they found nothing so hard in their life of travel from place to place as the making of fire. When camping for any length of time in a certain spot, one or two fires were kept constantly alight. In the first place they started the fire by friction. Some Indians, however, were in possession of flint stones. By holding one small flint firmly in each hand between the fingers and thumb, and against the stone in the left hand holding a small piece of punk or touchwood (a soft white or yellow substance into which wood is converted by the action of certain fungi, as *Polyporus igniarius*), and by striking these with the piece of flint held in the right hand a spark would be kindled which would cause the touchwood to catch fire and burn. With this and some dry sticks they would soon start a blaze. If they had no flint stones they had to resort to a much more difficult and tedious way of lighting their fires. This was done by means of a hardwood stick, hollowed out a few inches deep at one end, the other end being firmly planted in the ground. In this hollow cup the Indian would place a small quantity of powdered dry grass or touchwood; then with another and much smaller hardwood stick, held between the palms of his hands, he would by rotating it create a sufficiently high temperature to ignite the touchwood. Sometimes two or three Indians would be kept busy twirling the stick in the hollowed-out bowl before a fire could be started. This was usually the case during rainy weather. As soon as one Indian became tired out another would by placing his hands on the stick above or below the hands of the previous Indian, keep up the friction without a moment's pause. As the Indians had such difficulty in starting a fire, to the older and more responsible women would he entrusted the task of keeping it alight. And when moving from one place to another these old women would carry a lighted torch of wood, always watching to see that the spark did not die out. As soon as the camping-place was found they started one fire at least, from which the rest of the band easily lighted as many as they required.

Before the white man brought them kettles in which to cook they prepared their food by direct contact with the fire. The buffalo meat was ready for consumption after it had been dried, as the fires underneath the scaffold upon which it was placed served the purpose of cooking the meat as well as of drying and smoking it. When the Indians wished to boil water, they would dig a round hole in the ground, say ten or more inches in depth and six or eight inches in diameter, and into this they would fit a piece of coarse parchment or rawhide, securing it firmly around the top or outside part of the hole by small wooden spikes or pegs. This hole lined with the hide was water-tight, and after being filled with water several stones, heated as hot as possible, were dropped into it, one after another, until the water was brought to the boiling point. It was a very slow method, and was only used when steeping tea, boiling eggs or preparing food which required to be cooked but a short time.

Another method of cooking eggs, which they claim was a very good one, was by taking a short piece of a small green poplar tree, and carefully slipping off the bark, into which they put as many eggs as it would hold, or as many as they desired to cook. After building a fire they would bury this piece of bark under the hot ashes; but before doing so would close either end by a bit of the tree. The heat from the ashes soon cooked the eggs.

The few earthen vessels they did possess were usually taken from some of their enemies to the south, who seemed to have many more utensils than our Western Indians, and these were much prized as spoils of war.

Chapter 8

*• Signs and wonders • The naming of children • Peculiar reticence as to names •
The alternative • Premonitions and second-sight • The Northern Lights •
Ventriloquism.*

THE INDIANS WERE MOST SUPERSTITIOUS AND WERE always seeing signs and omens
in everything around them. This trait accounts for many of their peculiarities.
Their names were given to them as significant of some sign or happening which had
been taken as a warning. And if in after years some other important event happened
in their lives which they could convert into a sign it would be a reason for changing
the name given to them by their sponsors.

The naming of their children was a very solemn ceremony, and though very few
took part in it, the superstitions attached to the names given the boy or girl made it.
a very impressive occasion. The Indian who was asked to name the child would give
the matter a great deal of thought, and be more observant than usual to the happenings of everyday life. If a storm should come up, and perhaps be accompanied by violent thunder and lightning, the name of the child would have some reference to this,
such as "Four Sky Thunder" and "Lightning Shining out of the Clouds." If some particular bird had flown over the camp before the storm broke, the bird's name would
be included with the others, such as "The Black Hawk's Warning" or "The Bird who
Comes before the Storm." In after life the hawk was supposed to have a special
guardianship over the person who bore its name. In the same way the thunder or
lightning was looked to for protection from harm by the Indian whose name was in
any way associated with them. These names, given to him by some old and respected member of the band, very often indeed by the medicine men or women, the
Indian was never supposed to repeat. The mentioning of his own name, even most
solemnly, was supposed to imply disrespect to the powers of guardianship exercised
by the name, as well as being an unpardonable slight to the old Indian who gave it.
It is only in recent years that any Indian could be persuaded to mention his or her
name. It was, long ago, a most difficult task to obtain an Indian's name. He would
never mention it himself, nor would his wife, and his children would not dare to do
so. But the Indian or his wife would direct a person to some one else who would tell
his name, and even then one might require to use much diplomacy before getting the
desired information. This naming of an Indian after some bird or animal, or from the
elements, gave him his guardian or dream, Pow-wah-kun. And one of the prime reasons for never mentioning his name was that these Pow-wah-kunah were supposed
to be most sensitive, and were likely to do much more harm than good, if they were
ever shown any disrespect by their wards.

It often happened, however, that in after years a particularly noteworthy occurrence in an Indian's life would cause him to adopt some other name, and this name he could speak of at any time without fear of ill consequences. For instance, an Indian whose name given by his sponsors was "Star Blanket" might perhaps have been caught with one or two others in some very trying position, such as being surrounded by their enemies in some isolated place. The foe may have come upon them at daybreak and "Star Blanket" may have been the first to give the alarm, and in calling upon his friends to do their best, he might in looking up to the sky see an eagle, and would perhaps say, "If that eagle will help us by his strength and fleetness to escape I will take his name, and like him be strong and brave." Then, if they made good their escape that Indian would call himself "Kak-keeg-ca-way," meaning "The voice of an eagle." This incident is mentioned as an illustration, and, being an actual fact, is a fair example of the way an Indian would change his name late in life, and be known by it alone, while his first name, or the one given to him by his sponsors, would be remembered only by a very few. And the few who did remember it might by their relationship to him be in the position of never daring to mention it, for fear of some evil results to its possessor. One advantage of this custom of taking a new name later in life was the fact that the Indian's wife and relations could call him by it, and thus do away with a great deal of unnecessary confusion. If anyone wished, for instance, to find out to whom belonged some stray pony, it was most confusing to be told that it belonged to "Four Sky Thunder's sister's son-in-law's brother," this being the nearest approach to pronouncing a name by the average Indian. Whereas if the owner of the pony had adopted some name himself, one might be told that the pony belonged to "The voice of an Eagle."

In the naming of places the Indians often exercised their inventiveness, and frequently with highly poetical result. In a word or phrase they would describe the outstanding features of the landscape or commemorate some event or accident which occurred on the spot.

The most appropriate place-names in Canada are Indian names, and to assign to each and all their significance would be an attractive task.

There is much superstition and romance contained in the name given by the Crees and Saulteaux to the beautiful Qu'Appelle Valley. The Indians named this valley Ka-ta-pwa-wee-seeppi (The Calling River) because of the wonderful echoes heard along its banks and over its lakes, which they believe to be the voices of their friends and former companions in the Happy Hunting Grounds. The old Indians told many legends of the effects produced and the warnings given them by this echo. Probably none appealed more to their love of romance than the following:

Once many, many years ago there lived a chief of the Cree nation, much beloved by his tribe for his kindness and thoughtfulness and his good and wise counsel in time of need. This chief had an only son who was very brave, and ever first to volunteer for duty in scouting expeditions and raids. On one occasion the little band of scouts of which this young man, who was called First Son, was a member, was surrounded by an overwhelming number of Blackfeet, and most of the brave band were slain or wounded; among the latter was First Son. After the survivors had made their escape with the wounded they found that their leader would never reach the main camp in the valley, as his wounds were fatal, and one calm night in the month of June, which the Indians called the "Month of Young Birds," the chief's son started on his long journey to the Happy Hunting Grounds. As he was leaving them he bade his companions farewell, and told them not to grieve for him, because he was not going alone, for the young Cree maiden who was to have been his bride on his return to camp would accompany him. His companions left his body, which was wrapped in his beaded leather clothing, upon a scaffold, and with sorrowing hearts returned to the main camp in the Calling Valley.

After breaking their sad news to the tribe, and repeating the last words of First Son, they were told that on the very night upon which First Son had passed away, the maiden who had been watching for him insisted that she heard her lover's voice calling to her across the, lake; she had taken her little birch-bark canoe, paddled out to meet him, and had never been seen or heard of since.

The Indians imagine that in the echoes of the Qu'Appelle Valley her voice and the voice of her lover may be heard, mingled with those of others of the tribe who have passed to the Happy Hunting Grounds.

In this valley the "Barrier" is so called from the fact that here the Indians had built a barrier of stone to keep back the fish, and so sure were they of catching fish at this spot that they gathered salt to season them from the shores of the saline swamps which they passed on their journey towards the Barrier, fish being the only food that they could not eat without salt.

The Saskatchewan the Indians called "Kis-siskatchewan," which means Fast Running Stream, and Old Wives Lake was so called from the sad fate which befell three old Indian women, who with others of their tribe were being pursued by Blackfeet, and lost their lives while trying to cross the lake before they reached the ford. Ever since then, the Indians say, on the anniversary of this event they can hear the old women calling for help, and where the lake is very shallow they may be seen struggling in the water. The spot where the Qu'Appelle Valley joins the valley of the Assiniboine, the Crees and Saulteaux called Stony River, for here they first caught sight of the Assiniboines or Stony Sioux.

The Indians, who were always looking for signs, very naturally believed firmly in the spirit world, and had many experiences to relate of visits and warnings from their friends who had preceded them to the Happy Hunting Grounds. So firmly did they believe in these that many an expedition would be abandoned because some member of the band had had a warning of disaster overtaking the party. These were especially acted upon years ago when they were at war with other tribes. The warnings usually came to them in dreams, and they never hesitated to follow the advice of the Indian who told them his dream.

In many cases a relief party would be despatched to reinforce some expedition, on account of these premonitions; and they believed that but for such relief some calamity would have befallen their friends. There were times when this help came at a critical moment, which strengthened their faith in these warnings.

Not every Indian was enlightened by these particular warnings, but one or two in the band were supposed to be in some secret communication with the spirit world, and the word of these was taken as final when they predicted any coming event, either of good or bad fortune, to the members of their band. And in speaking of these Indians the others would say, "You know he is very wonderful, and not like the rest of us; the spirits commune with him. He can see far ahead." These spirits were also spoken of by them as dreams, or Pow-wah-kunah. Though every Indian of note had a Pow-wah-kun, they were not all honoured by this supposed peculiar intercourse with them.

The Indians also believed that in the reflection of the Northern Lights, or Aurora Borealis, was seen the dancing of the spirits of their departed ones. No Indian would whistle during the reflection of these lights, as some of the spirits might be tempted to return to earth if their friends whistled for them; and the return to this earth meant only trials and hardships for them. Whistling was believed to be the only way of communicating with the spirits of departed friends appearing in the aurora. It often happened after some victory of the Indians over an enemy that there would be a strong reflection of these Northern Lights, and this, they believed, was a dance of the spirits to celebrate the victory.

There have been among the Indians a few who practised the art of ventriloquism, and these were looked upon as being in very close communion with their Pow-wah-kunah. They would make the other Indians believe all manner of impossible things, and occasionally worked upon their superstitious natures to an astonishing degree. The last Indian known to have practised this art was an old Cree chief, "Loud Voice." This name was adopted by the Indian himself as soon as he discovered the fact of his being able to speak in this peculiar way. The Indians, not knowing anything of this art, very naturally looked upon "Loud Voice" as being a most wonderful old Indian. The old man never practised this way of speaking except during a thunderstorm, which added greatly to the uncanny effect of both storm and voice. He was a medicine man into the bargain, and though not a very successful one in the art of healing, was certainly more than successful in holding the respect of all the Indians of his band. But it must be said to his credit that he never used his powers to intimidate any of his followers, nor indeed any of the other Indians. But Ka-kee-she-way (Loud Voice) was a name to conjure with a few years ago among the Indian tribes, as he was known by hearsay, if not personally, to them all. This old Indian died at the Crooked Lakes Agency some years ago.

Chapter 9

• The love of children • Methods of training • Polygamy • Natural sensitiveness
and inherent dignity • Indian oratory • Poetry and satire.

INDIANS ARE OF A VERY AFFECTIONATE DISPOSITION, and also very undemonstrative. The love of their children was a particuarly pathetic trait in their natures. The youngsters were actually adored, and consequently would impress a stranger as being very badly brought up. They were never corrected for any faults, but, up to a certain age, did as they pleased, when, of their own accord, they seemed to realize the respect due to their parents. This was in a measure brought about by the way the older Indians treated the younger ones. No disrespect to elders was tolerated, and when the children were supposed to have reached years of discretion they were soon made to understand this, not by their parents but by other relatives and friends. Consequently the parents were spared the pain of correcting their children.

It was strange to note the peculiar change in some of these youngsters. They would have grown up having their own way in everything, and behaving generally in a most aggravating manner, yet a complete alteration would come in the course of a few day or weeks. This may be attributed to their very sensitive natures. For when a child was supposed, by the friends of his parents, to have reached the time when respect to his father and mother should be shown, he very soon was made to understand this by their treatment of him. He was told once or twice that he was no longer a baby to have everything his own way, and that it was quite time he should realize his position and try to help his father and mother a little more. If this advice was ignored, he was ignored also, and the rest of the band followed suit, so that the youth soon found the best policy was not to look upon himself any longer as a spoilt child.

The Indians very seldom had large families, the average number being five or six in a family.

There surely never were any happier or healthier babies than the little Indian "Awassisah." They actually appeared like little *voyageurs* from the first days of their existence, so sturdy and jolly were they. Shortly after birth the baby was tied up in the moss-bag, with its pliant wrappings of finely-dressed deerskin and quantities of soft moss, and a stiff leather support for the child's back. They were snug and comfortable in these bags, and safe from injury; and in the winter-time they were protected from the extreme cold by rabbit-skins.

The baby in the moss-bag made a compact bundle for the mother to carry on her back, wrapped in her blanket or shawl.

Chief Poundmaker, Cree, by Edmund Morris.

The moss which the Indian women used to wrap around the lower extremities of their babies was gathered from swampy lands in the vicinity of the spruce forests. When first picked it was in a variety of green shades, but after being dried it took on a peculiar tone of creamy brown and was a most hygienic wrapping for the child.

Some of the Indian women used a cradle to tie their babies in, and in the old days the women who had these were looked upon as possessing a luxury. The appearance of this cradle is familiar to everyone. No contrivance could so well meet the needs of the case. It formed a rigid, compact frame in which the child was held in safety through all the vicissitudes of the portage or trail. It could be swung on a tree or leaned against the wigwam, and the bow of wood extending above the child's head protected it from injury.

When the mother wished to carry her child she attached a stout leather strap to the top part of the cradle. This strap she then placed either over her forehead or shoulders, and away she would go, while the babe observed the passing scene or slept peacefully on, as he felt inclined.

The name "papoose" given to all Indian babies by the white man is the Sioux word for baby. The Crees called a baby "Awassis," and the Saulteaux, "Appinochi."

Years ago some of the chiefs and headmen had more than one wife, some having as many as six and even seven. It was surprising how well all these wives would agree. They called each other "sister," and might, indeed, have been sisters in so far as their fondness for one another was concerned. They divided their labours equally, and tried in every way to cultivate mutual forbearance.

The Indians had great respect for the aged, and for each other. They were very sensitive, and had to be treated with the greatest tact. Many a thoughtless remark was taken seriously, especially in the case of parents, who expected their sons and daughters-in-law to show them high and perfect respect. No idle jesting was tolerated from them. To such an extent was this carried that if a person took some remark made by his son or daughter-in-law to himself he might brood over it until it assumed unnecessarily large proportions. And he would leave the band or encampment for days and wander off by himself, only being appeased by an apology from the supposed offender. So it naturally fell to this person to follow his over-sensitive relative and apologize. The Indians as a rule spoke of their father or mother-in-law as "the person I respect."

Their manner one to another was always most considerate, their natural dignity making this treatment of each other very easy. They made excellent listeners, and never interrupted each other. This was especially noticeable at their council meetings and feasts. Each Indian would be given his own time to state his ideas upon the subject under discussion, and as his remarks were made standing, fully three or four minutes would elapse after he was seated before the next Indian arose to speak. If his views did not fall in with the others he would apologize, and perhaps make some jesting remark about his own stupidity, saying that of course he was known not to possess the brains of his friend who had just sat down, but if they cared to listen to him he would say his little say, and he trusted them not to ridicule him on account of his ideas.

The Indians expressed themselves in beautiful language. Their thoughts were poetical, and though they never made any actual rhymes or poems they had beautiful expressions. This may easily be accounted for, as they lived so much with nature and saw beauty in all around them.

They were fond of setting forth certain ideas by similes. For instance, one Indian, who is still alive and well known for his brilliant speeches, was once heard to say that he hoped the ideas he was about to express would not be as short-lived as the ripples which were made by throwing a stone into a perfectly calm lake. When the stone first dropped in it caused a sharp disturbance which formed a distinct but small circle, than one after another followed more circles, which, though extending much farther around than the first, did not leave so deep an impression, until they gradually lost themselves and the lake became perfectly calm again. The stone had been thrown in with a splash, which rippled almost over the whole surface of the lake, but after a few minutes there was no sign of it and it lay forgotten in the waters. Nothing ever came of it. He wished to speak seriously of things which concerned their future welfare, and hoped, if nothing came of his advice immediately, his words might bear fruit in after years and flourish. Let his words be as the tiny seeds which little birds carry away and leave in far-off lands. Here the seed grows as well as if it were on its native heath, and each year it brings forth fresh flowers, fruits or trees.

This speech was made in the Saulteaux language, and must have made a deep impression on all who heard it. The speaker possessed a low, musical voice which added greatly to the beauty of this expressive and poetical language.

There were certain speakers among the Indians who introduced a very cutting satire into some of their speeches. This was especially marked upon one occasion when the Indian first quoted had made a particularly flattering tribute to a certain educational institution, which was not appreciated by the old Cree Indian who spoke after him. This old man was also noted for his powers of oratory, and perhaps felt slighted at not having been called on first. But as he has always been most truthful and outspoken he may have only expressed his true opinions after all. However, on first rising to his feet to speak he said he was very sorry all the sugar had been used up in sweetening the previous speaker's words. There was none left to sweeten his tongue. The Indians years ago, when starting off to fight with their enemy, were always cautioned to keep their knives sharp—and from this came the saying, "May your knife always be sharp!" He didn't remember anyone ever having said to him, "May your tongue always be sharp!" but it was generally in that condition. With which introduction he began a scathing criticism of the methods employed by the white man to better the condition of his people.

Many other examples might be quoted of their way of expressing themselves, but the foregoing will illustrate their general style.

Chapter 10

• Hospitality • An Indian welcome • Friendly terms of address • No beggars •
Decline in good manners • Ingratiating speeches • Practical jokes.

F ROM THE EARLIEST ACCOUNTS OF THE MEETINGS BETWEEN the two races, the whites and the Indians, the hospitality of the latter has always been acknowledged. Every white man who came to them in friendliness found them most courteous and kind. When the Jesuit missionaries first came upon the Saulteaux, in 1640, they were kindly received. And again, years after, when Catlin spent some time among them he wrote most feelingly of their kind treatment of him. He travelled among the tribes who were noted for their warlike bearing, Indians who never hesitated a moment to face their enemies in times of war, yet he was received most kindly and hospitably, for he came as a friend, not as an enemy. With his two guides, Catlin was entirely at their mercy, and had they been of the savage nature so many writers have made them out to be they would never have spared him to write his letters, letters that speak so highly of all their good qualities.

The Indians have many phrases handed on for generations which show how easily they can express their feelings of hospitality. One of their favourite expressions when welcoming a stranger or a friend into their midst is "Ta-ta-wah," which means, "There is always room for you." Another expression when serving a visitor to a meal or any refreshment is "Kes-poo," meaning "May it satisfy you, or may it refresh you."

They never hesitated to entertain perfect strangers. As an example, if some friendly, though strange, Indian came riding into their midst, he would stop quite near the encampment and, after unsaddling his pony, would go into the nearest wigwam and be made perfectly welcome. After silently shaking hands with his unknown host, who always said something in the nature of a friendly greeting, they would both fill their pipes and smoke for a few minutes in silence, then proceed to introduce themselves. The stranger was never for one minute made to feel that he was unwelcome. In a very short time as many Indians as the tepee could hold would come in to make the acquaintance of the stranger, so that he would very soon feel perfectly at home with the whole band.

Years ago this stranger often proved to be "an angel unawares," as he might bring the news of the approach of an enemy, and perhaps save the camp from complete destruction. But it must be said to the credit of the Indians that it was with no idea of such reward that they entertained strangers. It was a pleasure to show anyone hospitality, and when they were in a position to do so they never thought of reward.

The Indians had many friendly expressions which they were in the habit of using when addressing strangers. They were usually terms of relationship, such as "Nes-tah" (brother-in-law), "Enjoe-wah-mish" (cousin). Nothing served to put the stranger so much at his ease as being addressed in this friendly way by his host and the other members of the band he was visiting. As a matter of fact, if a stranger belonging to the same tribe came to visit any Indians whom he had never seen before, they would soon manage to trace some real or imaginary relationship. They trace their kindred to wonderfully distant sources, and one might almost believe that the whole Cree nation was related or connected in some way. This may in many cases have been due to the way strangers were addressed by their hosts. Some one nearly related to this stranger would come some months after and claim relationship from this source alone, and this kinship was acknowledged without any question. Their natural consideration for each other would not permit anyone to disclaim this relationship. In this way one can easily understand the wide inter-relationship or connection existing among the Indians.

Perhaps few realize how hard it is for our Indians to have to beg for the common necessities of life. They are naturally very proud and reserved, and among the older ones to beg is most humiliating. Being brought up to look upon everything as for the "common good," it is hard for them to have to remind people by begging that they are in want. There is, as a matter of fact, no such word in either the Cree or Saulteaux languages as "beg." The only thing approaching such a word in their language is "Puck-oo-she-twan" (Share with me). A nation whose expressive vocabulary holds no such words as "beg" or "beggar" we should be proud to help if ever it happens to be in need.

Looking upon everything as their common property, they shared with one another all their belongings. Though some, of course, had more than other members of the band, none were allowed to be in want. They never asked for anything; their requirements were anticipated by the Indians who were in a position to give.

There is no doubt whatever as to the remarkable decline of good manners and polite usages among the Indians; years ago, everyone who studied their ways intimately was impressed with their natural dignity and fine manners. The Indian women taught their children certain things, but there were many customs which they seemed to acquire naturally and which only came from generations of dignified ancestors.

Then, again, not so very long ago there were many of the older Indians who were noted for their fine speeches; and these were pointed out as the remnants of what all the Indians had once been. A few of these tactful little sayings might be quoted just as an illustration. They were never addressed directly to the person for whom they were intended, but to someone near-by, thus avoiding any cause for embarrassment. For instance, if someone, especially a white woman, were introduced, the Indian would say, in acknowledging the introduction: "Now I know why the gods were good to me and spared my life till this day. They know how I love beautiful things," or "I have faced hundreds of our enemies without fear, and this pleasure is my reward." They would also say many complimentary things when they were speaking to each other. These remarks were usually made in reference to some brave deed or especial skill of the person whom they desired to please. They were most modest as to their own good points, leaving to their friends all expressions of praise.

Mustatem Moutiapec (Horse Roots), Cree.

There is no doubt that among the young men of the different tribes there was a certain amount of vanity and pride. But unfortunately for them there were also many wags who were ever ready to effect a cure for such cases.

The Indians, though always appearing so dignified and haughty, were nevertheless very fond of playing practical jokes on each other; all of which were taken most good-naturedly and returned in kind. They possess a very keen sense of humour, and some of their jokes were wonderfully clever and well-planned.

One has heard very often from the Indians themselves of the practical jokes which they delighted to play upon each other. Perhaps none was so popular among them in the past as that of a false alarm during the dead of night. When every Indian literally took his sleep with "one eye open" to prevent being surprised by the enemy this joke was very easily perpetrated; and the old Indians who are still alive take the greatest delight in relating the many ridiculous exclamations and antics of the startled and sleepy Indians. When the merry-maker was found out he had to be prepared for a return joke, and his life was not wanting in excitement until he had been paid back, with interest, for his work.

Sometimes a scout, coming upon friendly Indians, would wait until nightfall before approaching them, and without any warning would throw a stone into the middle of the encampment; whereupon every dog in the camp would set up the most hideous yelps and barkings, to the alarm of all the Indians. In a moment every brave would rush for his own particular pony and be prepared to do or die, when from the distance they would be greeted by some jocular remark in their own tongue from the author of the alarm. Perhaps they would be informed that the Blackfoot nation was sound asleep many hundreds of miles away, and that the speaker was very sorry that his sneezing had been mistaken for a fusilade of the enemies' guns, and in conclusion the speaker would remark that he was delighted to join a band of Indians who slept so lightly, as he was particularly in need of a few nights' rest at the time, and would be happy to leave the watching for the enemy to them. But, as stated before, this Indian would surely be paid back in full for his trick.

There were many stories such as these told by the Indians, and even if the joke was at their own expense they would enjoy relating the fun and merriment thus created.

Chapter 11

INDIANS WERE ALWAYS VERY FOND OF ENTERTAINING their friends to a feast of any decription, the most skilful hunter in the band being the one who usually furnished these entertainments. These feasts could not be classified as luncheons or dinners, as they were served at any hour of the day, from sunrise till dark. When the hunter returned from a successful expedition, bringing home with him some particularly dainty piece of game, he would have his wife or daughters cook every bit of it, and when the meal was ready to be served would invite his friends to partake of it. They had only one form of invitation for all occasions, for a council meeting, which usually ended with a meal, as well as for a feast. The host, standing at the door of his tepee, would call out the name of the Indian whose presence was desired, and say, "This is where you are wanted; bring your plate and cup with you, and also a good appetite." Some Indians would vary this form slightly by adding some remark, such as "Bring a good appetite; we may be able to furnish you with dishes to eat off, but cannot supply a good appetite."

The Indians thoroughly enjoyed themselves at these informal feasts, and during their progress would keep each other in continual merriment by relating all manner of stories, and as there were some very good story-tellers among them the repast was always a great success. The menu was very seldom a lengthy one, but the Indians managed very easily to make the meal last for an hour or two. After it was finished, the guests, before departing, would make many complimentary remarks on their host's skill in the hunting field and their pleasure in being his guests. These little flatteries were repaid, very naturally, by an invitation for some future occasion.

Council meetings were called by invitation of the chief or headmen of the band, and were only attended by the men of the tribe. Here were discussed matters pertaining to the welfare of the whole band or tribe. When things ran smoothly and the Indians were at peace no councils were called. But when game was scarce, as sometimes happened, or the winter season severe, they held these council meetings to consider the best way in which to meet these trials and hardships. Each speaker was given the closest attention and was never interrupted except by expressions of approval from those who were of his opinion.

During the tines when they were on the war-path, their council meetings consisted of discussions as to the best tactics to be employed in attacking the enemy. At such meetings any of the younger men who had shown some particular ability during an encounter with the foe were honoured by being called to attend. Here were decided the signals to be used by their scouts, and these were seriously considered, as being of so much importance to each band. They varied with each expedition or foray of importance, for they must needs be intelligible only to themselves, and the adversary was keen to become possessed of any code which would give his scouts information of intended movements. From long experience they had become skilful in elaborating their systems, which they successfully practised by means of reflections from mirrors, or some other polished or smooth article of wood or stone dipped in water to make it glitter in the sun by day, or by a bright fire at night.

They had also a system of signalling with smoke which they could practise with desired effect on dull or cloudy days. Each tribe had a secret sign which had to be given before any information could be exchanged between the operators. By these contrivances news was conveyed from point to point with a speed mystifying to anyone who was not aware of the significance of those glints of light or wavering shafts of smoke.

In time of war between any two or more tribes their scouts were ever vigilant and selected the highest hills or ridges from which to overlook the surrounding country and watch any movements or approaches of the enemy, and also to be in a position to convey information to their respective camps through their established or fixed chain of watchmen.

After the council was over the Indian who called it would invite them all to partake of some refreshment, and they would very soon be laughing and joking, seemingly forgetful of their serious conference of but a few minutes before.

The scouts were always chosen from among the younger men of the band. These by their powers of endurance and acts of bravery and cunning would win the confidence of all their friends, and were rewarded by being called upon to perform this duty.

After the scouts had been gone a few hours (or even an hour, when in the vicinity of the enemy) another little band of Indians would station themselves upon the highest elevation or hill near their camp and keep a constant watch for any signals from the scouting party. These watchers were relieved from time to time, and were in constant communication with the whole band, so it was almost impossible for an enemy to steal upon them unawares. It is easily understood, then, why the different tribes of Indians had so many skilled scouts; so much—in fact everything—depended upon their watchfulness.

The old Indians have many interesting stories to tell of their experiences while upon this duty. One old man told of a narrow escape he had had upon a certain occasion when he unexpectedly stumbled upon a hostile outpost. Sometimes the scout would have to leave his horse and go on foot to certain exposed places, where the foe might be seen. On this particular occasion he had tied his pony in the shelter of some scrub and was climbing up a steep hill near-by. As he advanced he got down upon his hands and knees and very cautiously crawled up to the very top in order to look down into the valley on the other side. Imagine his surprise when he came upon one of the enemy's scouts who had become tired with long watching and had fallen fast asleep. From his position he had evidently been looking out in the direction from which the Indian had come, but fortunately had fallen asleep before he had seen him. Now the narrator, finding himself in this position, knew that the minute his enemy awoke he would raise an alarm, and perhaps be the means of killing his friends, who had trusted to him for their safety. In an instant he realized that he must do away with his foe, and that without firing a shot, which would of course alarm the whole camp. Near-by was a good-sized stone, and this he managed to reach without wakening the sleeper, and it was only the work of a moment to despatch him by a well-aimed blow on the head. He left him there and, taking a careful survey of the valley and the encampment within its shelter, managed to get back to his pony and reach his friends without arousing the enemy. He soon returned with a small force and routed the foe. He, together with some friends, climbed the hill and buried the Indian who had, so fortunately for them, fallen asleep and been the means of their victory. With stones they made the figure of a man over the Indian's grave; and it is likely that upon that hill there still remains the memorial to an Indian who failed in his duty. The old Indian who told of this personal incident is still alive (1907), and in his day was one of the best scouts that the Saulteaux and Crees had. He was a splendid rider, had any amount of daring, and was an unerring marksman with bow and arrow as well as with the rifle.

The scouts had to depend many a time upon their bows and arrows, which in skilled hands were as deadly as firearms, and did their work silently. When a scout was surprised everything depended upon quickness and silence. If his adversary had time to raise an alarm by firing off his rifle or giving a war-whoop (which was an even more effective signal in such a case) the scout had small chance of escaping from pursuers as clever as he was in the art of tracking an enemy.

The favorite hero among the Cree story tellers is an Indian whose whole life was full of adventure. This Indian, who started life under the humblest circumstances, was one of the bravest of their band and was the pride of the whole Cree nation. Koo-min-ah-koush (Like-a-Pine-Tree) was a poor orphan boy brought up by his aged grandmother in as wretched a state of poverty as was possible among the Indians. At the time of his first appearance the Crees and Saulteaux were at almost continuous warfare with the Blackfeet, as well as with the Sioux. From the first this poor little boy (whose father had been killed by his enemies and his mother kidnapped by them) had heard nothing but talk of wars and raids. He was old for his years, being the constant companion of his grandmother, for whom he did as much as he possibly could. He seldom had anything new to wear, being clad in the cast-off garments of the children of his own size who were more fortunate than he. He never had any moccasins for his feet in the summer, and was altogether an object of charity and pity to the rest of the band.

His grandmother had three or four dogs, and these, with a travois, constituted their sole means of transportation when on the march. Koo-min-ah-koush, however, had learned to ride by herding the ponies belonging to different members of the band, and by even the youngsters who possessed their own mounts was acknowledged the best rider for his age. One can easily imagine how fond this little Indian boy became of riding, and how ambitious to possess a pony of his own. To his old grandmother he confided his few secret ambitions: to own a good, swift pony, to be a good shot with his bow and arrow, and to fight their enemies. The old woman was very clever at making bows and arrows, and it was her greatest pleasure to help her little grandson to fulfil one of his ambitions by furnishing him with one size after another as he grew up, and urging him to perfect himself in their use by constant practice. This he was only too glad to do, and with great success, as his future use of them showed.

His first adventure of note was at the age of eleven. At this time there were almost weekly skirmishes with the enemy, who were pressing upon them and following them north into their own part of the country. The Crees were encamped somewhere near the Saskatchewan River, where the city of Edmonton now stands. Koo-min-ah-koush had wandered into the tepee of one of the headmen of the band, who had called a council meeting. His presence was not objected to, as the Indians were only too anxious to teach the younger generation the arts of warfare, and the boys were usually encouraged to attend these meetings. At this particular one the Crees were planning an attack upon the enemy and arranging to send out a party of scouts early the following morning. There were to be five or six in the party, and these were chosen from their bravest men. Koo-min-ah-koush hurried to his grandmother's little tepee and begged her to get him a pair of moccasins and some buffalo thong for a lasso for catching horses. He informed her that he intended joining the scouting party which was leaving early the following morning. His old grandmother got him all he required, but warned him that he might not be allowed to accompany them.

However, the boy was determined, and started off with the party at daybreak the next morning. His presence was not noticed until they had gone some miles and had halted for a rest. Here the older Indians told him he must return to the camp, as his youth was against him, and he might by some blunder bring disaster to the party. He begged to be allowed to accompany them, and promised he should do nothing to cause them to regret his presence in their party. They would not hear of it, however, and told him he was nothing but a baby and had no courage or endurance. Then some of them actually taunted him with his upbringing by an old woman, who was hardly likely to have taught him the arts of warfare. Koo-min-ah-koush then hid near them and waited patiently all day long till the darkness made it safe for more scouting. Just at dusk a member of the party returned from a reconnoitre of the enemy's camping-ground. The boy overheard them plan the attack, and was ready to follow them when they started.

The party had decided to steal all the horses they possibly could without awakening the enemy, and if possible accomplish this without killing any of them. So they crept upon the sleeping camp, and each proceeded to cut loose a horse from the doors of the tepees where they were tied. The best horses were always tied near the door of the owner's tent, so as to be near at hand in case of an alarm, and also for the safety of the horses themselves.

But alas for their plans! The watch-dogs were aroused and by their barking gave the alarm. The Crees had already cut the lines securing the horses, and in this way managed to get a good start of their pursuers, but one of their number was slain. The boy, on account of his youth, had been unobserved, and by good luck had secured one of the fleetest horses in the camp, and riding away ahead of his party was able to get assistance from their own band, and himself led the way back to the rescue of the first scouting party he had ever gone out with.

This was the turning-point in his career. All the Indians had to acknowledge his bravery and endurance, and gave him every opportunity to fulfil his ambitions. He was soon recognized as their best scout, and he never returned from any expedition without bringing home some horses or other trophies of war.

He disappeared from the band when about eighteen years of age, only to return three years after with a complete mastery of the Blackfoot language, which made him invaluable as a scout to the Crees and Saulteaux. He had lived among the enemy and could pass as a Blackfoot. His achievements are thus summed up: "Koo-min-ah-koush was a great warrior and a strong medicine man. He killed fourteen Blackfeet before he lost his own life. His right eye was shot out by Low Horn in the fight when that warrior was killed. He was twice tossed by buffalo bulls, and each time severely injured; twice thrown from his horse, each time breaking some bones; and had three scars on his right side from Blackfoot bullets. It was thought by his own people, and even by some of the Blackfeet, that he could not be killed."*

One of his exploits is thus narrated: "On one occasion a party of Blackfeet surprised him with six of his young men, and drove them out on a small point of land on a lake. The Crees dug rifle-pits, and by firing from them kept the Blackfeet at bay all through the day. Night fell dark and cloudy, and Koo-min-ah-koush told his young men to swim across the lake, leaving their guns and ammunition with him, and he would fight the Blackfeet alone. After they had gone he ran from one hole to another, firing a shot from each, until his men had had time to get away. Then he crept out to the Blackfoot lines and began, like them, to fire at the deserted holes, and getting near to a Blackfoot he shot and scalped him, passed through the lines and escaped. In the morning the Blackfeet found the Crees gone, and only their own dead to look at."

Koo-min-ah-koush was a paragon of the Cree race and lived to be a very old man, dying near Fort Pitt in the sixties. Intrepid in war, he was noted in peace for his many acts of kindness, especially to the old women of his tribe, as he never forgot the grandmother who had cared for him in his youth.

Chim-ass-cous was another Cree Indian who was noted for his bravery. He was a medicine man, and at the time of his activity as a warrior, in the early part of the last century, was credited with having wonderful powers of second sight. All medicine men were not blessed with this power, and when one was supposed to possess it he was looked upon with much awe and honour by all other Indians.

The last expedition Chim-ass-cous led was when he was quite an old man, in the year 1851. The Crees had a large encampment at the Side Woods, a place southwest of Touchwood Hills, north of the Qu'Appelle Valley. Hearing of the approach of a band of Blackfeet, Chim-ass-cous suggested that a party be sent out to intercept their march northward into the Cree territory. He told his friends that after "making medicine" he felt confident of the successful issue of their raid should they start immediately and place themselves entirely under his instructions. It was never a difficult matter to secure volunteers for such expeditions, and Chim-ass-cous soon found his party large enough to warrant a start towards the enemy's camp.

* *The Story of the Indian*, by George B. Grinnell, pp. 107, 108.

They intended making a detour south of the place the scouts had reported, so they started for the elbow of the South Saskatchewan River and on to the Big Hill, which lay between Islet Hill and Ochre Hill. After sending out a scouting party from the Big Hill, the main body moved south to Ochre Hill, and, it being the early part of the summer, Chim-ass-cous decided to hold a Sun Dance (Nee-pah-quah-see-mun) while they were encamped there. It was an ideal spot for the ceremony, with good water and beautifully wooded. Their scouting party, being informed of the contemplated move from the Big Hill to Ochre Hill, were to join them in the dance. The scouts also, acting as bearers of an invitation from Chim-ass-cous, got word to quite a number of other Cree and Saulteaux, who joined the little band at Ochre Hill with the intention of taking part in the Sun Dance.

Unfortunately for them, a party of twenty or more Blackfeet had also been sent out upon a scouting expedition, and, by some peculiar chance of war, stumbled upon the dance at the Ochre Hill during the second night of its progress. The Crees and their friends, expecting the return of their own scouts, were most unprepared for a surprise, and were all intent upon their ceremony, when the party of Blackfeet rode into their midst. In a moment all was confusion, but they were not so excited as to forget to put out all fires and torches, thus leaving everything in total darkness. Chim-ass-cous and his friends had the advantage of knowing every bit of the ground upon which they had camped, and being unmounted, managed to overcome their enemy, as it was an easy matter to pick off the riders as they rode by and around the Crees, who, of course, had crouched upon the ground as soon as all the fires and torches in the camp had been extinguished. Some of the party escaped to the hill and signalled danger to their scouts, should they be in the vicinity.

The next morning the ground was gone over, and from evidence found Chim-ass-cous decided that their enemy of the night before had been a scouting or raiding party. They found the body of an old Blackfoot Indian with white hair, and as this sign of age is unusual even among the very oldest Indians, the place was renamed by them, "Where the white-headed old man was killed." From here they followed the few Blackfeet who had escaped, and overtaking them before they reached the main body from which they were an offshoot, managed to overcome a large number of them, and carried home many spoils of the fight, besides capturing an unusually fine lot of horses.

Chim-ass-cous remarked to his band of followers, as they wended their way back to the Side Woods, "I am an old man, and not white-headed. White hairs do not always mean success," referring to the old Indian they had killed during the night of their surprise. The Indians often use the expression which Chim-ass-cous used that day. For instance, if an old Indian has accomplished something out of the ordinary in hunting or in walking a long distance under trying circumstances, he may say: "I am old, but I can do more than one white-haired Indian did." Many such expressions have originated in just such a way as this one of Chim-ass-cous.

One of the peculiar incidents in connection with this expedition was the return of one of their scouting parties with the unwelcome information that they were being met by some of the enemy returning south from the Side Hills. This naturally caused a great deal of uneasiness among Chim-ass-cous' party, as almost every warrior had gradually joined them, and left in the camp with their wives and daughters were only very old men, almost unable to defend the camp.

The scouts had come upon the party at night on the return from their successful fight, and just one day's journey from the Blackfoot camp. All that night Chim-ass-cous prayed to Kichie Manitou (The Great Spirit) to give him second sight to see into the midst of the camping-party his friends had reported as being their enemy. The next morning he aroused his sleeping companions and informed them that instead of the approaching party being an enemy they were friends, traders from the Hudson's Bay fort at Touchwood Hills. And this turned out to be true, as they were shortly joined by the party of traders and induced to do some hunting before returning to their families at the "Side Hills."

It may, of course, have been possible that Chim-ass-cous had information of the intended departure of the Hudson's Bay traders at just such a time as would bring them to the vicinity of the Ochre

Pisquapita (Hair in Knot), Cree.

Hills when they were seen by the scouts. Be that as it may, the Indians always refer to this instance in particular as being one of the most wonderful in Chim-ass-cous' career as a medicine man.

Another Indian in whose prophecies of success or disaster in their undertakings the Cree and Saulteaux had great faith was "Kin-ah-cas" (You are leading), whose father was an Assiniboine and whose mother was a Cree. He was a great medicine man and was thought to have the help of very powerful spirits in his petitions to Kichie Manitou.

So successful were his predictions and instructions as to one of their expeditions that, upon the return of the victorious party, the chief gave him his young daughter to wed, this being the highest honour he could confer upon anyone.

Referring to the mixed parentage of "Kin-ah-cas," it may safely be said that some of their bravest men were the offspring of Cree or Saulteaux and Assiniboine parents. One of the Indians of such parents was "Piapot," who in latter years was looked upon as a great orator and a most courageous man.

A typical clash between two hostile tribes is preserved in a tradition of the fight between Yellow Head, a Cree leader, and the Blackfeet. It contains all the elements of desperate, sudden attack and intrepid, furious bravery which characterize their battles on the plains. This chief, with one hundred followers, returning from a hunting expedition and as yet many miles from the main camp, was ambuscaded by a war party of the Blackfeet. Outnumbered, miles from reinforcement, the light-hearted hunters, but an hour before sweeping along carelessly, laden with peaceful spoils, suddenly driven together became a band of heroes bound to sell their lives dearly. Skilfully and bravely commanded by Yellow Head, they fought for hours, beating back their assailants at every point and finally driving them off, but at what a cost! Yellow Head was killed, and sixty of the braves. The remaining forty, many of them desperately wounded, gathered up the horses of the force, and adding the trophies of war to the burdens of the chase limped, broken but victorious, into the astonished camp.

Chapter 12

• Poetry and music • Constant improvisation • The minor mode • No poetic or musical literature • The march song • Love songs • "The Calling River" • The farewell song • A boy's first song.

A PECULIAR LACK OF POETRY IS ONE OF THE FEATURES of the Indians' songs. Though they repeat words for the different tunes they sing, there is a lack of rhyme and rhythm in proportion to their naturally poetic language which is hard to account for. Each time a tune is sung new words seem to be composed for it, though, of course, they are always applicable to the particular song. In this composing or improvising of words for the different songs some Indians show very much more poetic feeling than others.

As a matter of fact, very few of their songs are sung to words except those which might be called love songs, and these, having once been sung by a certain Indian, are repeated by others, with a variation of words upon the original theme.

All their music is sung in the minor key. Even their festival music has a minor strain, especially when sung by both men's and women's voices, the latter always singing the harmony in the minor. It is hard to account for this peculiarity of their music, unless it be from their love of nature and solitude. The Indians as a whole are passionately fond of the pine tree, and anyone who has listened to the play of the winds in the pine forests will remember the strange minor moanings among the branches. It is more than likely that from this source springs their fondness for the minor strain in all their songs.

To most people who hear the Indian sing his different songs there is an apparent sameness in them all. But this is certainly not the case, as there are entirely different airs to each of their several songs, though all are founded upon one rhythmical *motif*.

One must always take into consideration the fact that the Indian had no way of writing down his thoughts. This made it impossible to have any poetic literature or any fixed traditional melodies. As has been remarked before, each Indian made up the words for his song, and these naturally varied when repeated by others, even though treating on a definite subject.

Their memory for the songs they sang was truly wonderful, and indicated a strong racial love for music. Take, for instance, the march song which the Indians used to sing on returning from a successful hunting or raiding expedition. Perhaps hundreds would join in the singing, yet every voice sang in most perfect tune and harmony.

Then as the party drew near the camp the women would join in, and they also were wonderfully correct as to time and harmony. The voices of the women were pitched in a higher key, and had a peculiar tone, resembling the notes of a flute more than anything else.

Each Indian composed his or her own love song, and the words were generally only suitable to one particular case, treating as they did of certain localities. Perhaps the valley of the Qu'Appelle ("The Calling River"), with its beautiful scenery, was responsible for most of their sentimental songs, the echo in the valley appealing at once to their fancy and superstition. One of the prettiest of the many traditions relating to the valley was that of the young woman who, imagining her lover was calling to her from one of the hills, pushed off in her little bark canoe and was never heard of any more. Her voice was left in the valley and answers back in plaintive tones when anyone calls. Her lover returned a short time after her departure, but, though he followed her, never found even a trace of her canoe. At twilight her canoe would appear for a few minutes upon the surface of one of the many beautiful lakes in the valley, only to disappear again in a soft mist if anyone tried to approach it.

This was a favourite theme for the Indian, and the tune to which the many different words are sung is most fascinating. In the olden days there was never an occasion of any importance which was not marked by its song. The meeting of a friendly band of Indians was always an occasion for singing. Their departure was also marked by its own farewell melody. When they were living peacefully, with no fear of the enemy, they passed most of their leisure time in singing and dancing.

It is a matter of regret that the Indians had no way of writing down or recording words and music. To many of them these are but a memory of happier times when upon every possible occasion they broke out into song. For them these times have gone, like the passing of the buffalo, never to return.

How proud the fond mother was of the first flight of song from her young son, and if she were fortunate enough to commit it to memory, she would often sing it when her son was away, hoping and believing its notes would be wafted through the dividing space and be a charm to protect him from harm and danger.

Chapter 13

THE INDIANS HAVE A MYTHIC ROMANCE WOVEN AROUND an imaginary being whom they claim to have been the first man upon this earth; a personage volatile and delusive, who has as many characteristics and attributes as vapour may have shapes and movements.

He is the pervading and ever-present Algonquin divinity, if the latter term be not too suggestive of worship to apply. He is called, among the Crees, Wee-sack-ka-chack; among the Ojibways, Nay-na-push or Nay-nu-boo-shoo. The Blackfeet know him as Napiw, or Old Man, the Micmacs as Gloos-cap; and he appears in the legends and tales of every branch of this wide-spread people from Nova Scotia to the Rocky Mountains and as far south as Virginia. Around him has been gathered, through ages, all the imaginative invention of minds given over to poetic and interpretative ideas, and his doings and sayings embrace everything from attempted explanations of natural phenomena to crude and often gross conceptions of humour. He has been treated as a "creator, a defender, a teacher and at the same time a conqueror, a robber, a deceiver." To a nature-myth Dr. Brinton refers his origin, a nature-myth representing, "on the one hand, the unceasing struggle of day with night, of light with darkness, and, on the other, that no less important conflict which is ever waging between the storm and sunshine, the winter and summer, the rain and the clear sky." But whatever the conception of this enormous and ever-changing figure, each Indian who in the days of the past had the gift of expression and the desire to create added to the store of legends his crude interpretation of nature or his tale of magic or adventure.

Wee-sack-ka-chack is represented as being a most wonderful personage, claiming to have created the earth after the flood and to have been the means of saving all the birds of the air and beasts of the field by his wisdom. He is also claimed to have understood and conversed with all the animals, birds, fishes and insects, and also with all manner of plants.

He was sometimes wonderfully wise, and upon other occasions most simple. He was tremendously self-opinionated and was always boasting of his attainments. This naturally made him try his powers upon all he came in contact with, and though almost invariably worsted in these contests, he never acknowledged himself beaten.

So wise did he consider himself that he looked upon everybody and everything as being much younger than he was, and insisted upon being addressed by them all as

A prairie encampment.

their elder brother, as an acknowledgment of the wisdom of old age. He never addressed anyone, or any bird, animal or plant, except as his "young brother."

Certain birds and animals who had treated him disrespectfully he punished by some peculiarity which changed their original appearance and was a lasting rebuke to all their kind forever after. There were others, again, whose appearance he improved, in return for some courtesy they had shown him.

The Indians say that all the ravines running from the tops of the mountains and hills into the valleys below were made by Wee-sack-ka-chack sliding down them instead of walking, as he was generally too lazy to walk down hill, and in many localities peculiar natural formations are pointed out as having been occasioned by some escapade of this ever-present, never-resting being.

There is a great deal of uncertainty as to where Wee-sack-ka-chack makes his home. The Indians say that for some reason or other he left these parts years ago and took up his abode on an island far away towards the rising sun (the east). They say if one were to walk till they came to the big water (Kichie-kamee) and were to look to the east they would see an island in the ocean; if they could get to that island they would see another much farther away, and upon that one it is supposed Wee-sack-ka-chack now lives. But when anyone lands upon the island he disappears from view and goes under the ground. He is so old that he has lost his good looks and is ashamed to be seen.

The Indians have a large number of myths relating to Wee-sack-ka-chack and his doings. There are usually one or two Indians in every band who are acknowledged to be good Wee-sack-ka-chack story-tellers. But they never tell any of these stories during the summer season, when they are, or should be, busy putting up stores for their winter use. In fact, Wee-sack-ka-chack himself made this rule, and in order to have it carried out instructed his young brother, the lizard, to keep careful watch that his instructions are observed. If they are not, the lizard must attack the story-teller when he is fast asleep and suck all the blood from his heart. So firmly do the Indians believe in this threat of Wee-sack-ka-chack's that it is impossible to get them to tell any of the stories during the summer, or, indeed, so long as there are any lizards in the autumn.

The following are a few of the stories which are told of Wee-sack-ka-chack. Two versions of the story of the flood are given. Almost every Indian has his own version of these interesting fables.

Once upon a, time, many hundreds of years ago, Wee-sack-ka-chack was warned in a dream that the earth was going to be submerged and the whole world was to be one huge ocean. He awoke from his sleep early one morning and found the whole sky overcast and showing every appearance of a heavy rain. He arose and made all possible haste to reach the very highest hill he could see. On his way he called to all the birds and beasts to follow him, as he was going to save them from drowning, telling them of the warning he had received in his dream. When he reached the hill he began to build an immense raft of large poles. In the centre of the raft he placed a tall tree with many branches. As soon as the raft was ready he told the birds and beasts to get on, as the flood might come at any moment.

Very soon it began to rain, and Wee-sack-ka-chack noticed all the rivers and lakes within sight begin to overflow their banks and cover all the surrounding country. All this time he kept calling to the birds and beasts to get on the raft and be saved, telling them if they did not do so they would surely be drowned. In a short time the waters had reached the top of the hill and the raft began to float away. There was no wind, only a steady rain and a dense sky overhead.

Many animals who had not reached the hill in time came swimming up to the raft and, resting their chins on the edge of it, begged to be taken on, which, of course, was done; Wee-sack-ka-chack was too kind to leave any of his young brothers to perish in the waters. As the raft began to fill, the birds had to perch upon the branches of the tree to make room for the animals.

The rain kept falling, and for many many days there was no break in the gray clouds above them, but the strange company upon the raft were kept safe from harm. Wee-sack-ka-chack kept count of the days by cutting a little nick in the tree which he had placed in the centre of the raft. When almost two moons had come and gone he noticed one morning that the clouds were beginning to break, and soon after the rain ceased. But even after the rain had stopped they floated about, driven first in one direction and then in another by the winds which came with the clearing of the sky. After a long time of weary waiting for the sight of land, Wee-sack-ka-chack decided to ask some of his little friends to help him find some earth, so calling the mink to him he said: "My young brother, we must try to find some earth, for if I do not make a new world for us to live in we shall all die. Now I want you to dive down as far as possible and see if there is any earth to be found beneath all this water." The mink jumped into the water and went down. After several minutes he came up almost exhausted and said he had seen no earth.

Wee-sack-ka-chack next called upon the beaver to investigate, but he too failed, after being gone several minutes. The otter was next called on, and Wee-sack-ka-chack urged him very strongly to try and go down far enough to bring up at least a tiny bit of earth. But the otter, too, met with no success, even after being down so long that he was almost drowned before they helped him on to the raft.

Wee-sack-ka-chack was at his wit's end to know which of his many little friends he could possibly get to go down next, when by merest chance he happened to catch sight of the rat; so addressing him Wee-sack-ka-chack said, "My little brother, you are a good swimmer and now our hopes rest upon you. Your big brothers have tried their best and failed; now you must go down: sometimes small things succeed where larger ones fail." So the rat dived off the raft and went to try his luck. He was down so long that all on the raft became very anxious for his safety. But presently he came up and was assisted out of the water by Wee-sack-ka-chack, who had great difficulty in resuscitating him. When he was sufficiently revived to speak the rat said he had seen the earth, but fainted before he could get any of it. Wee-sack-ka-chack was delighted with his little friend's success, and after a good rest sent him down again, asking him to do his best to bring some earth up with him. So for the second time the rat went down, and after a long time Wee-sack-ka-chack saw his body floating near the raft and had to pull him in with a branch of the tree. After they had worked over him for some time the fox noticed that the rat had his forepaws tightly closed as if holding something, and drew Wee-sack-ka-chack's attention to the fact. They opened his paws and in them found a little earth which he had managed to grasp before losing consciousness. Upon this earth Wee-sack-ka-chack started to work; blowing on it until perfectly dry, he scattered it a little at a time over the waters, and as he did so it began to form a solid mass which grew larger and larger around the raft until it looked like a huge island.

After a few days Wee-sack-ka-chack sent a young wolf around the land to report as to its size. The wolf was gone for only one day, and told his older brother that the earth was far too small for all of them to subsist upon, and if they were to live upon it it must be made very much larger.

So Wee-sack-ka-chack took some of the earth in his hands and scattered it so that it would be blown away by the winds to the four points of heaven. He then waited a few days before sending off another wolf to see the size of this island. This wolf on his return also reported the island as being too small for them all. Then again Wee-sack-ka-chack worked away and waited a week or two before sending another wolf to survey their land. This one returned in a year's time and said it was almost large enough but it would be to their advantage to make it larger. This Wee-sack-ka-chack proceeded to do, and after a month's labour sent out a young wolf, who came back after many years, an old wolf, with the welcome information that the earth was large enough for all the birds and beasts to live upon. It must be explained that every one of these wolves were sent early in the morning, just at sunrise, and they each started in the direction of the rising sun and kept on going around the island until they reached their starting-place.

As soon as Wee-sack-ka-chack was sure of the size of the earth he sent each animal and bird out into the world with his kind to make his living. It was here that he gave them all their names, each name being given on account of some peculiarity of its owner. And Wee-sack-ka-chack at this time also instructed them in the way each bird and animal was to make its living. For instance, he explained to the beaver how to use his tail as a trowel to build his dam. The beaver has done this ever since.

Because the fox was the first to notice that the rat's paws were closed tightly over the earth he had scratched up for Wee-sack-ka-chack, he was made more cunning than all other animals. Because the wolf had fasted longest when running around the earth, Wee-sack-ka-chack told him he would have the largest appetite for his size in all the animal kingdom. Because the skunk was not pleasant to come upon suddenly, Wee-sack-ka-chack put white stripes down his back so that people could see him plainly in the distance and avoid him. To the ermine he said, "My young brother, you are very pretty, but I think you will be prettier with a black tip to your tail"; and the ermine has always worn a tail with a black tip ever since.

Another version of a flood-myth and Wee-sack-ka-chack's connection with it is as follows: It seems that Wee-sack-ka-chack was the first person in the world. One day he started out for a walk, and after walking for a long time—almost around the world, in fact—he came to a hill. Now this hill overlooked a very beautiful valley, and in the valley he noticed a large wigwam. This he was delighted to see, as he felt sure some fellow-beings were living in it. But as he approached it he was surprised to see that the door was made of a wolf-skin. Wee-sack-ka-chack never killed any of his young friends, and did not understand why anyone else should have done so. But he was more surprised when he lifted the door of the wigwam and, looking in, saw two large snakes, coiled together and wriggling around. They actually appeared to make the ground upon which the wigwam stood tremble with their every movement. Wee-sack-ka-chack managed, however, to kill them, but being fascinated by their size and colour, he continued to gaze upon them till he noticed that they were gradually being submerged by water. He drew back from the tent door and looked around him, when to his horror he saw that the water was gradually rising all about him too. Pulling the wolf-skin off the door, he ran towards the hill from which he had seen the wigwam. The waters seemed to be rushing upon him, though he ran as fast as he possibly could. But when he reached the hill they appeared to stop, so he took fresh courage and, as he climbed, called out to all the birds and animals to come to him. When he reached the top of the hill he saw the waters were on all sides of him; then he knew that unless he made a raft immediately he and all his young friends would perish. So he cut down the largest trees he could find, and tying them together with the fibrous roots of others he soon had a huge raft built; in the centre of it he stuck a fine, straight tree with many branches. As he made this fast he said, "This is for my young friends the birds to perch upon. They can see a long distance from the top of the tree and can tell me if anything appears on the waters."

When the raft was finished he told all the birds and animals to get on it, as the waters would soon reach them and would cause the raft to float away from the hill. Very soon after this, rain began to fall in torrents and the raft floated away. A few of the animals who had not heeded Wee-sack-ka-chack's warnings to board the raft had to swim up to it, some being so exhausted by their exertions as to require assistance in getting on. While Wee-sack-ka-chack was helping some of them, others had to keep themselves from sinking by resting their chins upon the edge of the raft.

For days and days this strangely assorted company drifted over the waters. Wee-sack-ka-chack kept one of the birds upon the highest branch of the tree day and night, but none of them saw anything but water. It was during this voyage that the owl acquired the habit of staying up all night; as he could see in the darkness he was usually assigned to night duty. It was at this time, too, that Wee-sack-ka-chack came to know all the animals and birds so intimately. He had always been able to speak with them, but had not known them so well before this trip.

When the rain had ceased and the sky had cleared Wee-sack-ka-chack began to think seriously of their future and of how he was to make the earth for them all to live upon. They couldn't possibly live on the raft all their lives; so he called a meeting of all his young friends and discussed the best thing to be done. He assured them all that if it were possible to get even a tiny speck of earth he could from it make a huge island large enough for all. He reminded them of the fact that but for his love and wisdom they would all have been drowned, and that in return he expected their help in the present predicament. He wanted some of them to dive off the raft and try to bring up a little of the earth they had not seen for so many days. Three different animals volunteered to do this—the beaver, the otter and the rat. Wee-sack-ka-chack thanked them and said he would ask the beaver to go down first, as he was strong and accustomed to undertake very difficult tasks and was also a good swimmer. So off the beaver jumped and was under the water a long time, but on his return he had to confess that he had not seen a sign of any earth, though he had gone down very far.

The otter was the next one to go down. Wee-sack-ka-chack encouraged him to greater effort by reminding him that some of the best fishes were to be found in the deepest water. But though the otter stayed down much longer than the beaver he, too, disappointed his waiting friends by coming up without any earth and without having seen any.

Things began to look very bad for Wee-sack-ka-chack and his company, for the only volunteer left was the rat, whose size did not promise any better success for finding the material required to build a new world. However, the rat himself was most cheerful and seemed confident of being more successful than his larger and stronger friends, the beaver and the otter. Just before he dived off the raft Wee-sack-ka-chack impressed upon him to do his best, which of course the little rat had already made up his mind to do. They all watched him jump into the water, and waited most anxiously for his return. He stayed down for a very long time, and at last came up more dead than alive, but with the welcome information that he had seen some earth. Now this was indeed good news to them all. After a good rest he started once more for his seemingly impossible task. This time he was so long gone that his friends began to fear for his life, because even a rat cannot stay more than a certain time under the water. However, one of the animals suddenly noticed his small, limp body in the water, and Wee-sack-ka-chack managed with the aid of a branch to pull him near enough to the raft to get him on board. He appeared to be dead, but Wee-sack-ka-chack worked over him until he felt his heart begin to beat and knew he was going to live. Just then the fox remarked that the rat had his paws tightly clenched, as if holding something, so Wee-sack-ka-chack forced them open, and sure enough the brave little fellow had managed to scratch up some earth in each small paw and had thus saved the situation.

Wee-sack-ka-chack took the earth and dried it very carefully. Afterwards he blew it in all directions, and wherever it fell the land began to form. After days of this work Wee-sack-ka-chack thought he had surely made an island large enough for them all, but in order to be sure of the size of his island he looked around among his friends to find one who would run all around it and report as to its size. Some of the animals were a little nervous about undertaking this task, but Wee-sack-ka-chack said to the wolf, "Now, my young brother, you are surely brave enough to do this. Remember I saved your skin from the door of the snake's tepee, and in return you must do this for me." So off the wolf started, running toward the rising sun, and in that direction they waited for his return. He was only away for a year when back he came, saying the island was not nearly large enough. This report started Wee-sack-ka-chack again, and after working for weeks he sent off another wolf. This one was away so long that he was old and grey when he returned. He said the island was now quite large enough for them all. Wee-sack-ka-chack was delighted to hear this, and said to the wolf, "You may be old and grey, but you will be game to the last, and you shall be able to fast longer than all other animals, and also to eat more than any other of your size when there is food to be had."

Chapter 14

ONCE UPON A TIME WEE-SACK-KA-CHACK, on one of his numerous travels, had to climb to the brow of a high hill. It was a warm day in the month of Moulting Birds (July), and when he reached the top he was very hot and tired and sat down to rest himself.

Presently he noticed two huge eagles soaring far above him, and he called to them, "My young brothers, come down and let me get upon your backs and take me up high into the air where it is cool. I am tired and very warm." So they came down, and, letting Wee-sack-ka-chack mount upon their wings, they bore him up towards the sky and the swaying motion soon lulled him to sleep. Imagine his surprise when he awoke to find himself shivering with cold, and up among the clouds. He at once told the eagles they had taken him too far up, and to carry him down to the earth again. But this they had no intention of doing, and instead kept going up higher and higher until Wee-sack-ka-chack found himself in a region of huge icicles which seemed to be suspended from the heavens. To save himself from striking against them he grasped one in each hand, and found himself deserted by the eagles and hanging in the air.

The warmth from his hands soon caused the icicles to melt, and the cold water from them trickled down his arms and body. He realized that it was only a matter of a few minutes until the icicles should be melted by his hold upon them, and calling to the eagles, who had remained in the vicinity, he begged of them to come to his rescue. But those unkind birds left him to his fate and saw him drop down into space. Poor Wee-sack-ka-chack was going down and down towards the earth, which appeared to be miles below him. He had lots of time to think, and also to pray, during his travel through space. So he made supplication to the earth that she might be kind to him and guide his fall to some one of the many soft places on her broad surface. The earth heard him, and guided his flight to a soft mound, where he fell. But the force of his fall caused him to be buried almost to the middle of his body, and as he came down head first his trying position may be better imagined than described. However, he managed to extricate himself by wriggling, and when he did get out was completely exhausted and lay down in a semi-conscious condition. He was aroused from this state by feeling some crows pecking at him, and hearing some wolves arguing among themselves as to whether he was alive or dead. He was too weak to speak, and lay quietly gazing up towards the heavens, when he saw the two huge eagles hovering above him. This helped to bring back his senses, and he said to the crows, "My young brothers, I am not dead yet, but stay around me and pretend to be picking at my flesh. I want to punish those two eagles when they come to eat me." So the crows did as requested and were soon joined by the eagles.

Wee-sack-ka-chack lay on his back with his arms stretched out and his palms open. Very soon the eagles began pecking at the palms of his hands, and awaiting his chance he suddenly closed his hands upon the eagles' heads and held them firmly. After struggling for a long time they managed to get away, but left all the skin from off the tops of their heads in his hands.

As they flew away, Wee-sack-ka-chack said to them, "You and all your descendants will evermore be bald, for having treated me as you did in causing me to fall from the sky."

And the Indians say that Wee-sack-ka-chack's words were fulfilled, and all the descendants of those two eagles have carried the unmistakable mark of his displeasure; to this day none of them have any feathers upon their heads.

Once upon a time, when Wee-sack-ka-chack was very hungry, he started out to find some food. As he walked along he came to a beautifully-situated little lake, in which there were a number of geese. Now it suddenly occurred to Wee-sack-ka-chack that there was nothing he desired to eat so much as a goose. In looking around for something with which to kill them he spied a peculiar hollow-centred reed, from which he could produce a strange, weird music which appealed to all kinds of birds and wild animals.

Procuring a few of the reeds, he began to play upon them; the geese had no sooner heard it than they waddled out upon the shore and came towards him. Wee-sack-ka-chack with his usual cunning pretended not to see them, but continued playing. Very soon he had all the geese dancing around him in a clumsy but rhythmic measure. He kept up the music so long that the geese began to get quite tired and were unconsciously narrowing the circle in which they danced till they were actually pressing up against him. With his disengaged hand he twisted their necks one after another as they came to him without arousing any suspicion among them. All shared the same fate. Wee-sack-ka-chack was delighted with his success, especially as none had escaped to tell of his work. He was always anxious to pose as the friend of all birds and beasts, and would not for worlds have his true character become known to them.

After gathering up all the dead geese he carried them to a spot near-by, where he soon built a fire with which to cook them. When he had burned sufficient wood to make quite a heap of ashes he buried all the geese under them. He arranged the geese in such a way that though their bodies were completely buried, their legs and feet stuck out of the ashes. This was to help him find the birds when they were cooked. To hasten the process he made a good big fire over all the ashes, and then went for a walk in order to sharpen his appetite.

As he walked along a sly old fox caught sight of him and said to himself, "My friend Wee-sack-ka-chack has a most self-satisfied expression this morning; he must have had a successful hunt. I wonder which of his young brothers he has played some trick upon to-day." When he saw Wee-sack-ka-chack approaching in his direction he pretended to be fast asleep.

Catching sight of the fox, Wee-sack-ka-chack went up to him and said, "Well, my young brother, you have had a good rest, so should be fit for a race with me to-day. I am feeling very well and am sure of winning. Will you run a race around that little lake with me?" The fox said he was perfectly willing to try conclusions with his older brother, but could not very well do so just then as he was suffering from the effects of a sore foot. Wee-sack-ka-chack, of course, believed all this, and offered very generously to handicap himself by tying a stone to his ankle and also giving the fox a few yards start of him in the race. The sly old fox very reluctantly consented to this arrangement and the race was started. As soon, however, as they were out of sight of each other the fox ran as fast as he could and presently came to the fire which Wee-sack-ka-chack had left a few minutes before. He at once proceeded to investigate and soon discovered what was cooking. He made short work of all the geese, and before leaving buried all the feathers and carefully arranged all the legs and feet of the geese in their former position. He then started off to finish the race and reached the starting-point long before his old friend had gone half the distance. He lay down to rest, but after his hearty meal was so drowsy that he very soon fell into a heavy slumber. Wee-sack-ka-chack at last reached then end of the race, and much to his surprise found the fox ahead of him and fast asleep. He at once became suspicious, as the fox was in the habit of playing just such tricks upon his elder brother, so he examined each of the fox's feet and, as he suspected, they showed no signs of cuts or bruises; but in the kindness of his heart he concluded to let his young brother sleep, while he went on to enjoy his dinner. He felt sure that the geese were sufficiently cooked for him by that time and hurried on, only to find that the fox had eaten every one of them and had concealed the trick most cleverly by putting each pair of legs back just as he had arranged them.

Wee-sack-ka-chack then returned to where he had left his unkind friend fast asleep, and, gathering a lot of dry grass, made a complete circle with it round the sleeping fox; then, setting fire to it, he sat down and watched the flames burn up. The heat very soon awakened the fox, who jumped up, hopped over the fire and got away, remarking as he went that his "older brother was a very good cook," which reminded poor old Wee-sack-ka-chack how very hungry he was, more especially as he had anticipated such a hearty meal.

But, with his wonderful powers of endurance, he started out again with a will to get another meal.

He had lots to think of as he trudged along: of the many tricks the fox was always playing upon him, and of those played on him by the different birds and other animals. Then, again, he thought of how he had ill-treated so many of his young friends. He realized that he had not treated his friends the geese fairly himself that very morning, but he excused his conduct by thinking of the intense hunger from which he had suffered, and, as he said to himself, they were not asked to dance, even if he did make such appealing music, and if they had stayed in the water they might all have been alive now. But we shall see whether staying in the water would have saved them.

After he had walked quite a long way he came to a very pretty part of the country, hills and little inland lakes everywhere about him. He sat down to rest, and as he did so imagined he heard the splash of ducks or geese in some near-by lake. Presently he heard a goose honk quite near him, and this was too much for poor old Wee-sack-ka-chack, who started out in the direction from which the sound had come and soon discovered a lake in which were fully a dozen or more of his young friends. The sight of these made Wee-sack-ka-chack feel very hungry and reminded him of the meal of which the fox had deprived him. He sat down by the shore of the lake and began crying out to the geese in a most pitiful tone to come near him, as he wished them to help him out with their natural enemy the fox, who had treated him very badly. When the geese came near he asked them to turn him into a bird, as like themselves as possible. This the geese agreed to do, so very soon Wee-sack-ka-chack felt his body being covered with feathers and wings sprouting out at his shoulders. He tried to fly, and only managed to get out a few yards into the lake when he fell in among the geese. The geese warned him not to try flying for a few minutes longer, as his wings were not strong enough to carry him. He followed this advice and explained to the geese why he was so anxious to fly. He wished to catch up to the fox, and asked them to accompany him and help him get rid of their cunning enemy.

After waiting for some time the geese told Wee-sack-ka-chack his wings were ready, and to lead the way, which he was only too glad to do. As he started off in a certain direction the geese told him not to go that way, as they had seen a wigwam and were afraid they might be shot by the occupant if they passed over or near it. But this was exactly what Wee-sack-ka-chack desired, so he kept on in the same course, explaining to his companions as he flew that the wigwam was occupied by his young brother, who would not touch them. Very soon they came in sight of the wigwam, and Wee-sack-ka-chack began honking like a goose; this was for a signal to his friend in the tent, who came out at the sound with bow and arrow, and, taking aim, shot at the passing geese. Alas for Wee-sack-ka-chack's calculations, instead of one of his companions being shot, he found to his horror that it was his own wing that the archer had found. He came tumbling down, and the geese immediately hurried away, making good their escape. As Wee-sack-ka-chack fell, he found himself at the door of the tent, without a feather upon his body, which surprised his friend very much and was also a surprise to himself. He tried to explain his masquerade as a goose, much to the friend's amusement, who chaffed him upon his success and reminded him that he should have appeased his hunger as the geese did while he was one of them.

But Wee-sack-ka-chack did not stay to hear all his friend had to say, as he was quite determined to get a meal for himself before the sun had set, so, borrowing a bow and arrow, he again set out.

He travelled for some distance without seeing anything he could try his skill upon, and, becoming very tired, sat down to rest. As he rested he looked around and was struck with the excellent quality of the grass which grew around him, saying to himself that "as the deer and buffalo ate grass and grew fat upon it, why should not he have some of it?" He felt sure the sun would set and find him as hungry as when he first started out in the morning. Getting up, he went to a particularly green place and began picking up some grass with the intention of eating it.

Now we know he understood all languages and could speak with all animals, birds and fishes, so he also could speak with and understand all plants and trees. As he picked the grass up, he said, "My little friend, I am very hungry and must eat you, though I should much prefer some of my little friends who are in the habit of eating you." The plant answered him and said, "My older brother, you must not eat me. I am only intended for the food of your little friends. If you eat me you will not be able to kill anything with your bow and arrow." But Wee-sack-ka-chack only laughed and said, "My young friend, I must eat you, for I am hungry." After he had eaten a few blades of the grass he started forth again on his hunt. Presently he reached a beautiful valley, and to his delight he saw on the opposite hill a group of four jumping deer. He managed to get quite near them and, adjusting his bow and arrow, took aim and shot. But alas, his arrow refused to go farther than a few feet and the sinew string of his bow made such a peculiar squeak that the deer were startled and ran over the hill and out of sight. Wee-sack-ka-chack was reminded of the threat of his little friend, and, realizing that he had not been satisfied in the least by his eating the grass, began to regret very much not having taken its advice and waited for more suitable food with which to appease his hunger. However, he thought he would try his luck once more before going back and apologizing. Very soon he came upon some more deer and again tried to kill one, but with the same result. He turned back to the spot he had taken the grass from for his meal, and, reaching it, began to implore the forgiveness of his little friend, and asking to have restored to him once more his cunning with the bow and arrow. He promised never again to eat any plant not intended for his use. The little friend then said, "Go, my big brother; you always make us believe that you are wiser than any of us, but you see even wise men sometimes make mistakes and turn to the most insignificant for aid."

Wee-sack-ka-chack soon after came upon the four deer he had seen earlier in the day, and to his joy succeeded in killing one and satisfying his hunger. He did not forget his promise to the little plant, for he never allowed anyone to eat of it again. That is why no Indian ever eats grass. There are many things they learned through the experiences of Wee-sack-ka-chack, and this is one of them.

Index